G

10 Keys to Taking Control and Living a Happier Life

David Nelson

ISBN: 0-9710858-0-3

Cover design by Jonathan Gullery

FIRST EDITION

To my family and friends for their patience
as I learned—
and continue to learn—
life's lessons.

Table of Contents

Introduction

The following advice is designed to help you take control of your life and increase your personal happiness. If you are up to the task of living a happier life, you have come to the right place!

This book contains what I believe are the 10 keys to a happier life. I chose them because they all have two fundamental requirements: universality and simplicity. Universality means that they apply to everyone, everywhere. Simplicity means that they are easy to remember and easy to apply.

One thing you must realize from the start is that I guarantee that you have heard at least half of the keys. But hearing something once, twice, or even a dozen times does not mean you will embrace it and act accordingly. You may even say, "I know that" to all 10 keys. If you do, remember that I am not here to tell you anything you *don't* know. I am here to help you do the things you know you should do, admit to the ways you get in the way of your own happiness, and then change those ways, thereby increasing your personal happiness.

What I need from you . . .

As of this moment, consider us a team. My intention is to help you as best I can. In order for you to optimize the effectiveness of the information in this book, I recommend you create the best environment to do that. That environment has very specific requirements, all of which should be present in order for you to get the most from this experience.

This is what I ask of you, and what you should do for yourself:

- Be honest with yourself. You know when you are trying to scam yourself, and you know that no one does it better than you.
- Keep an open mind.
- Be willing to examine your life.
- Be receptive to suggestions.
- Read the stories and learn from them.
- Note (but don't react to) the actions and reactions of others toward you; they are telling you something.
- Embrace the idea of change; it is good.
- Desire to reach for your potential.
- Get comfortable with the idea that you have made mistakes and you have been wrong in the past. Both will happen again.
- Don't sell yourself short—plenty of people will be glad to do that for you.

The 10 Keys to Taking Control and Living a Happier Life are:

1. Happiness is a Decision
2. If What You Are Doing Isn't Working, Do Something Else
3. Accept Other People

4. You Can Recreate Yourself at Any Time

5. Life Is Reasonable

6. Draw the Right Picture

7. Before You React, Consider Intent

8. Give What You Want to Get

9. Communicate

10. Believe

You will find that there is a theme that runs through this book, and that theme is what will help you take control and be happier. If I do my job right, I will help you understand that your life is a continuous stream of choices, many of which are directly responsible for what happens in your life.

Once you acknowledge and take responsibility for your choices, you will experience the reality that you have more control over your personal happiness than you previously thought. And that other people have less to do with your personal happiness than you previously thought. Take responsibility for the choices you make – it is the first step in taking control of your life and an essential part of every key for living a happier life.

The First Key

Happiness is a Decision

You probably are not as happy as you could be. And I'm certain that you are not as happy as you *should* be. The First Key to a happier life—Happiness is a Decision—is the most important in that it reminds you that you have control over your state of mind. My hope is that after you have read this book, whenever you are feeling that things have spun out of control and you are not content with where you are, you will recall this First Key. You will remind yourself that Happiness is a Decision, and you will instantly examine what you are thinking, saying and doing that has contributed to your situation. And you will alter your thinking, your language and your actions so that you quickly recover. It really can be that simple.

But if you are not yet convinced, you are not alone (my evidence? All of the miserable people in the world). The concept that Happiness is a Decision is not a popular one. I have observed a phenomenon that I think is unfortunate: It seems as if people are becoming increasingly more focused on placing blame. And while this blame is well placed at times, we almost always play a role in what befalls us through the choices we make. If you are not a believer, examine this stream of logic:

- You can change the way you feel by changing the way you think and changing the words you use.

- When you change the way you feel, therefore, it is because that is what you have chosen to do.

- You can choose to be happy, sad, angry, or resentful.

- So if you are not happy at any given moment, and you have the power to change the way you feel, happiness becomes a decision you have control over.
- Likewise, and crucial to this notion, is that if you are unhappy, on some level you have chosen that feeling.
- If being unhappy isn't working for you, decide to be happy.

How? The Big Secret Revealed

The big secret in the contentment industry, of which I am a spokesperson, is that the keys to living a happier life are not big secrets at all. Like Dorothy in the heel-clicking scene at the end of *The Wizard of Oz*, you already have the keys to what will make you happy. But also like Dorothy, those keys might be buried so deep inside of you that you do not know you have them. There's an old saying that goes: I'll believe it when I see it. My experience has been the opposite – you'll see it when you believe it. In other words, when you believe something is possible, it is much more likely to happen. Happiness is a Decision, and making that decision is a lot easier than you think. The only thing in your way of making that decision is you.

If you have been behaving a certain way for most of your life, that way is what you know best. And although the process of changing is not always easy (and I'll discuss that process later), the initial decision to change is quite simple. Just do it. Say, "I choose happiness from this moment forward." There. Done. Wasn't that easy?

And now for the hard part . . .

In order for your happiness to manifest into more than words, you probably need to examine the ways in which you subvert your happiness every day. Once you become aware of the ways you sabotage yourself, you can choose to behave in a different way, one day at a time. I personally guarantee you that each day you choose to think and act productively and in a positive way will make you a happier person. Let's look at several of the fundamentals of thinking and acting positively.

Work Toward Rather Than Away

As I see it, there are two motivators in life: avoiding a negative and achieving a positive. I think you'll agree that the higher motivation is to go toward something positive. Happiness is definitely something positive, so you're on the right track.

What is Your Role in Your Unhappiness?

Once you embrace the notion that your feelings emerge because you allow them to, you create a bit of a quandary for yourself. When you realize how much control you have over the things that bother you (by assuming control of your thoughts), there's no room to complain about how victimized you are. Liberating yourself from the shackles of your own negativity is such a satisfying feeling that you will be amazed that you ever allowed you to get the best of you.

When you truly understand that you alone are responsible for the way you think and feel, and you decide to act in ways that express that responsibility, you'll realize that you can never again utter the following words to anyone: "*You make me feel (angry, sad, guilty).*" I'll discuss more about this in The Sixth Key.

> *Mandy and Terrance were very much in love. Mandy always bragged to her girlfriends that she found a man who wasn't like most men. Terrance was sensitive and gentle, showered his wife with affection and gifts, and called her his Dove.*

Mandy and Terrance both had fulfilling, full-time careers. The home routine they developed was that Terrance would come home, change into more comfortable clothes and watch television. Meanwhile, Mandy would come home, prepare dinner and then clean up after dinner. Periodically, Terrance would come into the kitchen to refresh his ice tea, smile at Mandy, make a sincere comment about how good dinner smelled, give Mandy a peck on the cheek and then head back to the TV.

Mandy would clean the house and do the laundry on the weekends, while Terrance would play baseball in the local over-30 league. Mandy didn't particularly care for baseball, and besides, this allowed her time to clean the house without having Terrance underfoot. I'm sure you know what happened.

Eventually, Mandy began to resent this scenario, dreading how much more she would have to do when they had children. Mandy and Terrance had very busy lives, but when Mandy compared what she was doing that made her busy to what made Terrance so busy, she was not very happy. She slowly became enraged with Terrance and began complaining to her girlfriends, who all had similar stories. She discovered, from talking with her girlfriends and her mother, that the reality of marriage is that women do the majority of the domestic chores, in addition to the childrearing. And many work outside the home, as well.

One day, when Mandy and I were having lunch, she unloaded all of her complaints about Terrance. This is what transpired . . .

Mandy: (after explaining what an "inconsiderate nimrod" her husband is) "Can you believe this? It's like, he really is a stereotypical guy after all!"

David: "Wow, Mandy, do you mean to tell me that you guys had a discussion about the household chores and who would do what, and then you discovered that your part was too much, and then you told him how you were feeling, and then you asked him to chip in more, and he still has the nerve to not change anything about his behavior? I don't believe it either!"

Mandy: "Well, that's not exactly what has happened. I mean, we never really talked about it, but it's not like he isn't aware that he comes home everyday and plops himself in front of the television while I have to take care of everything even remotely related to tidying up, and then make dinner and clean up."

David: "Have you told him that you think this is unfair?"

Mandy: "I shouldn't have to tell him. Any normal, intelligent, considerate person would realize that maybe he should clean up after himself and offer to help me out once in a while! During my adult life, I have never made anyone clean up after me! What did he do before he met me?"

David: "I don't know. What did he do before you got married? I mean, did you spend much time at his place?"

Mandy: "Sure I did – I was there a lot. It was a lot of fun. Terrance would be cramming for finals and I'd come over after work and make him a nice dinner. He would study while I helped him pick up around his apartment."

David: "So, before you got married he used to help you more around the house?"

Mandy: "Well, mostly he studied and I picked up."

David: "So you haven't said anything to him about how things are now, right? You haven't actually asked him to do anything?"

Mandy: "Like I said, I shouldn't have to. If he really loved me, he wouldn't do this to me. I would never treat him so inconsiderately."

David: "Yeah, but you didn't marry yourself, you married him. Let's back up; I'm still a bit unclear about all of this, Mandy. You say that he "makes you" do all of this, and you say he is "doing this to" you. You mean to tell me that he tells you that you have to pick up his suit or else? And does he tell you to make dinner and clean up or he'll . . . Are you being physically abused? Is that what you're telling me? I can't believe this either! He doesn't seem like that kind of guy at all!"

Mandy: "No, no, no, calm down. Terrance is a loving, gentle person and has never even raised his voice at me."

David: "So what has he done to intimidate you into doing everything around the house?"

Mandy: "Intimidate? He's not the least bit threatening."

David: "So what's the problem? Boy, I wish I were him. Why do you do all of that stuff? Who says you have to do it?"

Who has the problem and what is it?

The problem is really Mandy's: She is refusing to accept responsibility for her own misery. A pattern was established, with two willing participants, where Mandy does most of the work. The moment she felt overwhelmed, taken advantage of, or the least bit resentful, she should have said something. No one should expect anyone else to read their mind. *If you are angry, you shouldn't expect your partner to figure that out and then guess why.* The only people who are allowed to do that are infants, and that's because they have not yet developed the language skills necessary to tell those around them how they feel.

Mandy sounds like she is accusing her husband of doing something terrible to her. Meanwhile, he probably has no idea that she believes he has done anything wrong because her behavior hasn't changed and *she hasn't told him how she feels.*

I don't want to turn this into a discussion about gender and housework, but the reality is that in the majority of marriages, the woman does more of the housework (and child-rearing) than the man. However, this reality, and any other situation of inequity, will only change when both parties take responsibility for their roles.

Though Terrance's behavior certainly does seem inconsiderate, it is what I call Passively Inconsiderate (and I'll discuss the concept later in The Seventh Key), meaning that he is not intending any harm or distress. In fact, he probably hasn't given a thought to the whole situation.

For me, the most interesting aspect of relationships involving a Passively Inconsiderate person, is that the actual problem that results (and certainly all of the angst) really lies with the partner. The partner is the person affected by, and usually infuriated with, the Passively Inconsiderate person. So in Mandy and Terrance's case, not only was Mandy the upset party, but she was at least half of the reason why she was upset.

Why do I say that? Because she was a willing participant in the creation of the routine that she eventually resented. The moment Mandy felt angry, she should have said something. And not just anything. There are some reactions that could do more harm than good, regardless of how appropriate they seems to be at the time (to the person saying them). One such reaction might be: "Why do I have to do everything while you sit your lazy, good-for-nothing butt on the couch everyday, without so much as an offer to help me with anything or even a 'thank you' for everything I do for you?"

My advice? Sarcasm begets sarcasm, and while many people think that kind of banter is entertaining, it ends up causing problems the moment one person starts to take it more seriously, or personally, than the other intended.

How about: "*Honey, when you choose to watch television rather than clean up after yourself or help me with dinner, that tells me that you do not appreciate me. I choose to do the things I do for you as part of my expression of my love for you. I am feeling like I do a lot of work around the house, and it has been making me increasingly unhappy. I would like you to chip in more than you do; that is something that would be a way you could express your love for me.*" Such a statement from Mandy would be an expression of her acceptance of her reality. And it would be a healthy step toward resolving the problem that she is having.

Getting Angry With Reality Is Not Productive

When people get upset it most often results when their reality does not match the expectations they had for what would be, just like Mandy from the above story. A lot of the time, we act as if the problem is reality, but the *reality* is that the problem is often our expectation. For instance, I want to go to Home Depot on Saturday morning and I don't expect to wait in a long line. Now, if I've never been to Home Depot before on a Saturday morning, no one can fault me for this expectation. But if I have been to Home Depot on Saturday – and have experienced the busyness and long lines, then it's not too bright of me to go with an expectation of not waiting in line, wouldn't you agree?

If I took a moment to examine the reality of the situation (i.e., that most people work on their homes on the weekends because that is when they have the time and energy to do so, and that most people would like to begin—and finish—as soon as possible), I would be able to guess that one of the busiest times at Home Depot is probably Saturday morning.

Taking those couple of moments to think through the facts of a situation often saves you a lot of time and energy being disappointed when your unreasonable expectation isn't met. If, after careful consideration of the facts, I decide to go to Home Depot on Saturday morning and I am met with a long line, it was not Home Depot that inconvenienced and disappointed me and caused me to become frustrated by waiting in line. *It was me, for having an unreasonable expectation!* Although I'd like to blame Home Depot or all of its inconsiderate customers for my inconvenience, the fact is I got exactly what I *should have* expected.

If I decide to go to Home Depot again early on a Saturday morning, I should accept the reality that there will probably be a line, and bring my Walkman or a book and keep myself occupied, or even productive, while I wait on the inevitable line. And I have no business acting shocked, dismayed or angry.

While out shopping on Christmas Eve this past year, I found myself in a long line behind a woman who appeared to be very frustrated. Talking to no one in particular, I heard her say: " I cannot believe these lines! What is the deal here?" Our conversation proceeded as follows:

> *David: "Is this your first time shopping on Christmas Eve?"*
>
> *Frustrated Shopper: "Are you kidding? No, I'm a last minute kind of person. In fact, I don't recall not shopping on Christmas Eve!"*

David: "So, you shop on Christmas Eve every year, eh? Are there lines like this every year?"

Frustrated Shopper: "Oh yeah, and every year it frustrates the heck out of me."

As I continued to wait in line behind the frustrated shopper, I couldn't help thinking: This woman has shopped on Christmas Eve for years, has experienced these lines for years, and yet still stands here frustrated and angry about a situation that she *knows* has existed for years! Even her choice of words is astounding to me: "I can't believe these lines."

"Really? If I recall correctly, you just told me that you've experienced this for years and yet here you are surprised to find that it's the same way it's always been? DUH!" No, I didn't say all of that. But I wanted to.

Essentially, this woman chose to shop at a time when she knew full well that there would be long lines, and yet she was upset about it. This makes no sense to me; it's a complete waste of energy. YOU are responsible for the informed choices you make. It makes no sense to choose and then complain!

Speaking of waiting . . .
Is it wrong to be late?

Robin is a thirtysomething woman who is rarely on time for anything. She is not in denial about this and structures her life, as much as she can, so that it does not become an issue. She has even chosen a career that allows her to work from home, so her career has never been jeopardized by her chronic lateness.

But her marriage of six years is a different story. Her husband, Mike, whose primary way of coping is humor, has developed enough jokes about his wife's lateness to fill an entire evening of stand-up comedy. His favorite one revolves around Robin even being late for their first date. His friends always bet against his wife arriving somewhere on time, and he always takes her side, hoping each time that this will be the time she is able to be prompt. After all, he is thinking, I keep talking to her about it and telling her that it upsets me.

Robin has improved somewhat and is good about choosing obligations where timeliness is not truly essential. However, she is still late about half the time.

Mike has reached his threshold and is so upset with Robin's lateness that he has raised the topic of divorce. Mike, by the way, is rarely late. Robin is shocked that Mike is so angry, considering the fact that, for as long as they have known each other, she has rarely been on time and has actually told him to bet against her when he gets the opportunity. According to Robin, she doesn't plan on being late, but "one thing after another happens, or I am suddenly stuck in a heap of traffic, and before I know it, I'm late."

Mike thinks that Robin is wrong, and that if she really cared about their marriage, she would train herself to be punctual.

My question has three parts:

1. Is it wrong to be late?
2. Who has the problem?
3. What is the real problem?

I'll start with the third question because I think it's the easy one. The real problem is that Mike is unhappy with *the reality* that Robin is not a punctual person. Each time Mike is supposed to meet Robin, he has a choice: He can accept the reality that she will be late and plan accordingly, or he can refuse to accept the reality that his wife has always been late and will continue to be late, and he can choose to get angry every time.

Essentially, Mike has chosen to be angry with the reality that his wife has a trait *that she has always had – from their very first date!* He is angry with her for being, well, her.

So is it wrong to be late? Apparently, for Mike it is, but for Robin it isn't. The solution? Given the positives of the relationship that Mike and Robin have, is Mike willing to accept the reality that he has always known about and never liked? If so, he should stop complaining about that reality and acting utterly surprised when it arises. He doesn't have to *like* the reality that Robin is always late, but he has no business expecting her to magically become a punctual person when she has never shown any inclination to do so.

The Balancing Act: Weighing the Positives and the Negatives

Like Mike, when you are feeling dissatisfied with a relationship, you must do something about that in order to honor your feelings and respect yourself. I suggest making a list, mental or physical, of the positives and negatives of the relationship. Your decision won't necessarily be based on which side has more items, as items differ in quality and importance.

In addition, your list is only accurate *up until the moment you wrote it*; you don't have to act as if the list cannot change. You can request a change or propose a compromise, if that is what is necessary to make you feel satisfied in the relationship.

You cannot control other people, only your reaction to them.

Mike spent an awful lot of time being angry with Robin for being who she is (i.e., different from him and not able to live up to his expectations). Where did that get him? Think about past events in your own life that upset you. No matter how upset you got, did that change anything?

One of the gifts God has given us is free will: the means to make decisions (and I'll discuss free will further a bit later). Being upset is one of those decisions. So is being happy. In every situation, before you rush to judgment or to a reaction, take the time to examine the facts, make informed decisions, examine your role (did you have reason to believe beforehand that there was a possibility it would be like this) and don't complain about the results. If you do not like your results, learn from them (i.e., don't make the same decision, under the same circumstances again) and move on.

I'm an advocate of remembering the way you felt after you made a decision that was not well thought out. That kind of reinforcement helps you create positive changes. But focusing on the fact that you made the bad decision is a waste of time. Just think of your bad decisions as opportunities to learn and grow. Focus on the lessons your experiences are offering you, for that is where the value lies.

The Second Key

If what you are doing isn't working, do something else

I'd like to introduce this chapter with what is perhaps the quintessential perplexing question about life: *Which came first, the chicken or the egg?* The egg, right? I mean, that's where the chicken comes from. Oh, um, yeah, I guess it was probably a chicken who laid that egg, so that would mean the chicken came first. Right? Maybe?

Okay, how about this one . . . Which came first, thoughts or language? If you said thoughts, think about this: How do you have a thought without some kind of language? I am not referring to speech, because as we all know, there are plenty of people who successfully communicate without vocalizing. Communication is merely the usage of a system of symbols that we agree represent the various aspects of our existence. But if you said that language came first, why would it have developed unless there was a need for it? Why would it have developed unless someone *thought* about wanting a system for communication?

Think way back to the cavemen. At some point, caveman #1 *thought* about attempting to communicate with caveman #2. Perhaps caveman #1 wanted to enlist the help of caveman #2 to hunt down some dinner. So there he is, caveman #1, *thinking about* asking caveman #2 for help. What did that thought look like? Was it an image in his mind? Whatever it was, it was some form of language, of *representation*. But how would you know you had a thought if you couldn't somehow represent it, even to yourself? A bit like the chicken and the egg, wouldn't you say?

The language vs. thought conversation has been going on for years, and is part of disciplines called Linguistics and Semiotics. Although there are some questions that Semiotics and Linguistics probably will never answer, they do help us understand our relationship to language.

We know, for instance, that words really aren't anything without people. Words, by themselves, mean nothing until some people agree on what they mean; they are largely arbitrary. A chair, for example, is a chair because we have agreed that chair is what it will be called. The word chair (as a noun) brings something specific to mind because you have been trained to associate a certain structure and function with the notion of chair. The details, such as the size, color and style of a chair, differ from person to person, but the basic idea of a chair is consistent regardless of which English-speaking person you ask about a chair. The same is true for the word lamp.

But not all words are that simple. Take love, for instance. What is it? Does it bring an image to mind? Does it make you feel something? Furthermore, do I define love the same way you do? Should I? The less concrete the concept is to begin with, the more room there is for individual differences in definition.

However, no matter how different your precise definition of love is, if you were to repeat the word love to yourself in your head, something would happen. The feeling or image you associate with love would immediately come to mind. Essentially, the word would cause a feeling to occur. It also could have introduced thoughts that weren't in the forefront of your mind. So it is the catalyst for thoughts as well as feelings. The same is true for all words that you have learned to associate with pleasant emotions (and all words that you have learned to associate with unpleasant emotions).

Language=Thought

Language and thought are so inextricably related that you can change the way you *think* by changing the language you use. And language and feelings are so connected that you can change the way you *feel* by changing the language you use.

Think Your Way to Happiness

Your thought process is largely responsible for the way you feel. So if you are feeling miserable, the thought process you are currently using is partially responsible. It makes sense, then, that if you want to change the way you feel, or create a specific feeling, you can enlist your trusty English language to help you. You have to change the way you are thinking if you want to change the way you are feeling.

My only caveat is that precision is very important, and the old adage holds true: Be careful what you ask for, because you will get it. It may sound simple, but the most important thing you can do is to think before you speak. You probably *think* you already do that, and maybe to an extent you do. What I am suggesting, however, is to think about the words you plan to use before you launch them out into the world. Or, more importantly, before you say them to yourself. Consider each word literally, and ask yourself if the word you have chosen best expresses what you want to say (I'll delve more into this in The Fifth Key).

"But I've tried that in the past and it hasn't worked!"

Sometimes, try as you may, you have difficulty changing your thinking and behavior. When that is the case, it could be due to the reality that a negative thought process has been so ingrained in you that you no longer recognize it. And if that's true, using your current thought process to change your mood or behavior is probably not a very productive strategy. But don't fret; there is a Plan B. Think of your golf swing for a moment. Or your tennis serve. Better yet, read about my pal Erwin.

> *Erwin is an avid golfer and his swing has never been satisfactory to him. He has videotapes of himself swinging his golf club, and it is obvious that his problem lies with his grip. Erwin knows what he has to do to improve his swing, so he goes to the range a couple of days a week after work and hits golf balls. After a summer of practicing and practicing, Erwin's swing didn't improve at all. In fact, I'm no expert, but Erwin's swing appeared to have deteriorated over the summer.*
>
> *Erwin's wife suggested that Erwin enlist the help of Eric, a golf pro who taught her how to swing a club. "Why?" Erwin scoffed, "I already know how to do it, I know what I'm doing wrong, and I know exactly what I have to do to fix it." Erwin's wife pointed out that he had just spent three months "fixing it," and to the best of her knowledge, he wasn't even close to successful.*
>
> *Naturally, Erwin wasn't receptive to his wife's commentary and she immediately tried to rephrase. "Erwin, Eric told me that the number one reason why people who are trying to improve their golf game don't improve it, is that they don't seek professional help. He said: 'Everyone thinks they can do it on their own. Everyone except the pros. You don't see Tiger Woods assuming he can fix his game without consulting Butch Harmon (his coach). A difference between the pros and amateurs is that the pros want coaching, while the amateurs think they don't need it.'"*

If you have tried, in earnest, to alter your thinking and your behavior by altering your language, and you have yet to make any progress, my advice is to get another opinion. If you have ever seen a therapist, I probably don't have to tell you how enlightening and entertaining it can be. But if you haven't seen a therapist, and particularly if you are someone who thinks therapy is only for "crazy" people, you might want to look one up.

Here's why: It is possible that you are so mired in the muck of your current thought process that you think you are changing, but you really aren't. A therapist is a *trained*, fresh ear who doesn't have the baggage you have (they have their own personal baggage, designed just for them) and will hear and react to your exact words. It is possible that you are so close to yourself that you do not see yourself, or hear your words realistically.

If what you are doing isn't working, stop wasting your time!

You have a finite amount of energy and it should be directed toward positive, beneficial things. If you are spending a lot of time and energy in areas that you are unable to affect, you are wasting your time. Rather than continuing to create your own discomfort and unhappiness, change the way you operate. Get over it and create your happiness! What good does it do to get upset? It is a learned behavior and it doesn't take you anywhere good. You've probably been perfecting all of your unproductive and dysfunctional habits for years. Now it's time to unlearn them by changing the way you handle the everyday events of your life.

Your First Step

As you know, feelings tend to have a way of creeping up on you and infiltrating your consciousness. Sometimes you are suddenly overcome by a feeling of sorrow, anger, or even love. If the feeling you have is one you do not want, you have the power to change it. Furthermore, if something occurs that has historically provoked certain feelings in you, you can choose to not allow it to affect you. *But you need to own up to it first.*

What I mean is that you have to examine whatever situation you are in that you are unhappy with, and *find* at least one thing you can do to change it. There will be many things you cannot change, but some things you can, and your first step is to separate them and concentrate on the ones you can change.

Sometimes you will be certain that you cannot find anything that you can change . . . .

When Rae was 45 years old, she took a position as an advertising executive in Manhattan. This was her fifth position of this kind since she was 30 years old and had just finished her MBA. She had a beautiful apartment and made a decent living. She traveled abroad each year and dined out at chic restaurants several nights a week.

There were several women Rae's age working for the same company: some in administrative positions, some in her position and some in top-executive positions. This was true at her previous five companies as well.

Rae was a fine worker and never had trouble with her colleagues or superiors. The problem was that, at 45 years of age, she was suddenly overwhelmed with the realization that she was not happy with her career. For the first time, she began examining the jobs of the top executives and wondered why she wasn't one of them. Clearly there was no glass ceiling, as plenty of women held top positions. She concluded—as any intelligent person would—that there was some kind of conspiracy keeping her from achieving success.

When Rae reached her conclusion and said it aloud to herself, she immediately knew she had to rethink it. The facts were that she knew she was at least as smart and good at her job as the women who were promoted. She rarely worked over time and didn't even work that hard because everything came easy to her. In fact, her jobs were so easy that she often helped her bosses and colleagues with their duties, and she had a reputation as a helpful, competent, super intelligent, friendly person.

As far as Rae knew, she had been received the same way since her first day in the workforce. "But if I am indeed as wonderful as they claim," she asked herself, "how come I am not a top executive? Why do I keep getting stuck in these middle-of-the-road positions?"

What took Rae 15 years to realize was that even though she was doing well by most people's standards, she was capable of so much more and was not even attempting to live up to her potential. She said it herself as one of the facts of her situation: she didn't work that hard because everything came easy to her. She was coasting along, as she remembers she did all through high school, college and graduate school. She never tried, yet she always experienced some level of success. Rae had to admit that her unhappiness began long before her current job, and even long before her career began.

Rae was face-to-face with her history of complacency and had to acknowledge that she was the sole party standing in the way of success beyond her imagination. And the reason was that she never took her imagination seriously and never admitted that deep down, she wanted more for herself.

Rae managed to turn her image around to one of a mover and shaker with higher ambitions. After her first review, she was given a larger territory, which meant the possibility of increased income. Within two years she was a top executive and she was happy. And her happiness didn't come from her position, it came from inside her. It was so simple: all she had to do was decide that she was worthy of more, and then go get it.

If the heart of your problem is an emotion . . .

If your emotional state is unpleasant, what you are doing is partially responsible. There are plenty of unfortunate circumstances in all of our lives. And when they begin to pile up, it is very easy to feel unlucky, victimized and depressed. This too can change . . .

> *14-year old Mackenzie was devastated when her 11-year old retriever, Cody, was diagnosed with cancer. Cody had several operations, the last of which was the partial amputation of one of his legs.*
>
> *Mackenzie cried frequently for several weeks. When Cody was brought home after his partial amputation, Mackenzie was deeply saddened because Cody would never be able to play and run like he did when they were growing up together. Every time Mackenzie looked at Cody she couldn't be happy. And every time Cody tried to walk, Mackenzie would cry at his attempts. She was so empathic and depressed that she no longer had an appetite and all she would do everyday after school was lie next to Cody and cry. Cody stopped trying to walk.*

Anyone who has had a pet for a long time has experienced some kind of illness and loss, and we all know how painful it can be. And when there is a child in the family, the situation is compounded, as many children are very attached to their pets.

Mackenzie and Cody's story is really about the reality of loss and the tendency of some people to empathize to the point of utter misery. Mackenzie's parents eventually talked to her about the reality that crying all day about Cody was not going to change anything. In fact, she was probably making the situation worse because she was treating Cody as if he were already dead. They explained that if she wanted to, she could decide to help Cody learn how to walk. They told her that there are plenty of animals and people who are differently-abled and who live happy lives.

Mackenzie's parents made her promise them that if she was going to come home from school everyday and spend every moment with Cody, she was going to do it with a smile on her face. And she wasn't allowed to lie next to him, either.

If she was going to spend all of her time with him, it would be productive time, and her mission would be to help Cody learn how to walk.

Mackenzie contacted the vet to ask her how to help Cody. Mackenzie learned all about Cody's cancer and his surgeries and aided in his healing and rehabilitation. Cody participated enthusiastically and learned a new way to walk.

Misery is a Decision

There's a saying that goes something like this: If you keep doing what you've always done, you'll keep getting what you always got. This is especially true of the way you handle your unpleasant emotions. There comes a time when being miserable no longer serves any purpose. Not only is it not effective, it is destructive. This is even true with the grieving process.

Concentrating on what can be done rather than crying over what cannot be changed is a positive, productive response to any unpleasant situation. If you find that you are spending your time and energy perpetuating negativity, try a different tack. You are certain to get different results. The next seven keys will explain the seven things you can begin to do, today, that will help you on your journey to taking control and living a happier life.

The Third Key
Accept Other People

In my opinion, you cannot begin your journey to happiness until you can focus on yourself. And by focus on yourself, I don't mean in a selfish way. What I mean is that you need to stop looking all around you for reasons why you are not as happy as you'd like to be. You need to stop blaming others and stop trying to change them. Remember that your happiness comes from you and the decisions you make. Just as you chose to be happy in The First Key, you can also choose to claim responsibility for your role in whatever you think is causing your discontent.

Most people would say that they already accept people for who they are, they don't judge anyone, they don't have unreasonable expectations of anyone and they don't expect anyone to act the way *they* would act. And most people are fooling themselves. Only themselves.

Perhaps you can relate to this story . . .

40-year old Stefanie lives in Connecticut and her widowed mother Frances lives in Florida. Stefanie has a husband and twin toddlers and her in-laws live in nearby Massachusetts. Since the twins were born, Stefanie and her family have spent their holidays with her in-laws. Months before each holiday, Stefanie extends an invitation to Frances in Florida, so she will have plenty of time to get a flight for a reasonable price. One November, Stefanie called Frances . . .

Stefanie: "So mom, the deal for Chanukah is that we are going to the in-laws for the week, and there's plenty of room for you, so you can come for the whole time, for just a couple of days, or whatever. Just let me know."

Frances: "Do you realize that for two years and a dozen holidays and birthdays I have been expected to come to you if I want to see my grandchildren?"

Stefanie: "Of course I realize that, mom, but I just don't want to travel with them yet. Car trips are enough of a nightmare with them—you have no idea!"

Frances: "May I remind you that I raised three children, practically by myself, and at holiday time I did whatever was necessary to get you three to see both sets of grandparents and no one even had to ask me."

Stefanie: "But things were easier for you—your parents and your in-laws were just hours away!"

Frances: "It doesn't matter. If I was in Connecticut and my mother was in Florida, I would pay her the respect she deserved and I would have packed up my three kids, rain or shine, and showed them that all of their grandparents matter. I'd teach them to value their grandparents . . ."

From what I heard, this conversation went on for quite some time and was never resolved. The problem here is that there is no right and wrong. Stefanie doesn't want to travel with the twins but also gives Frances ample opportunity to see them. Meanwhile, Frances declines *out of spite*, and is infuriated. And the source of Frances' anger is that her daughter is not behaving *like Frances would*. Frances is angry with Stefanie for not being more like her. Further, she has exaggerated Stefanie's real reasons (difficulty and distance) to the level of disrespect, when they were really quite reasonable.

It would take so little energy for Frances to get a ticket and fly up to Connecticut, as thousands of Floridians do every holiday. But her self-righteousness keeps her from seeing her child and her grandchildren. And until she accepts Stefanie and the decisions Stefanie chooses to make, Frances probably won't be seeing her grandchildren.

Frances needs to establish her priority. Is it to spend time with her family? While it should be, it certainly seems by her actions that her priority is to see if her family—people she supposedly loves—would go to great expense and difficulty to prove that they respect her.

Frances Isn't Alone

I think we all would like people to be the way we want them to be (or better yet, the way we are). Naturally, we assume that our way is the right way, and if someone is not doing it that way, they are wrong. Changing this idea will go a long way toward improving your relationships and your state of mind.

You Can't Change Your Family

Stefanie and Frances' situation is a good example of one of the most difficult dynamics of many people's lives: their nuclear family. For some reason, we all grow up thinking that we can "fix" or change our families. We also assume that we *know* exactly what is wrong and that we have the *power* to fix it. Think about that for a moment. Isn't it just a wee bit arrogant and presumptuous?

For many people, "family" conjures up memories of Thanksgiving dinners gone bad (and I'm not referring to the food). Then there's the Christmas when you couldn't wait to get up on Christmas morning, *because that would mean you were that much closer to leaving*. Family, for an unfortunate (large) population, is not a positive image.

If you are one of those people who have had years of (or even just some!) negative experiences with your family, where you would define family as "the place to go if you want to get annoyed," there is an alternative. It is the best kind of alternative: one that you have complete control over. *Get over it.* And the first step toward getting over it, or anything else, is by answering a simple question.

Do you have any faults or weaknesses?

No? None at all? Oh, a few? Yeah, me too.

In order to accept other people, warts and all, as they say, you must first accept yourself. And that self-acceptance begins with a willingness to admit your weaknesses. Right now, think of your two biggest weaknesses. And that doesn't include the ones you use at job interviews such as, "I am almost too responsible" or "I learn so quickly that sometimes I can't even keep up with all of the things I know." I am referring to real weaknesses: traits that have gotten you in trouble at least a couple of times. For instance, impatience, greed, dishonesty. Make it count.

You'll work on doing something about your faults in a short while, but for now, just like you declared: "From this moment on, I am a happier person," say your two faults aloud. Your wording should be: "In the past, my biggest weaknesses were (fill in the blank) and (fill in the blank)." You word them as such because you want to tell the universe that those faults were the you of the past. The phrase "I am greedy" sends a far different message from "Up until today, my biggest weakness was that I was greedy." Think about it.

When you hear yourself declare your weaknesses, an interesting phenomenon usually happens: you realize that you are just as human as everyone else. You make errors, and sometimes the same errors over and over again. You have faults, and sometimes those faults are the first thing you notice about other people.

How do you feel about the possibility that other people don't expect or want you to have any faults? Don't you think that's a bit unreasonable? In fact, don't you *expect* other people to cut you some slack and realize that you have faults?

Doesn't it seem fair, then, that you should give them some room to make errors? Isn't that both realistic and reasonable? The Eighth Key: Give What You Want to Get discusses this concept further.

Now, about those two big faults of yours . . .

Do you want to change your faults? If so, decide to do just that. The best way to do that is to describe your new self and start becoming that person right now. As you will see, you can decide what you want to be from the moment you think you are acting like someone whom you don't like.

The Fourth Key

You Can Recreate Yourself at Any Time

Who are you?

This is no small question to begin this discussion with. Maybe I should start with an easier one . . .

Who do you really want to be?

And I'm not asking you if you could be anybody, who would you want to be? I'm not looking for answers such as: Bill Gates, Julia Roberts, Kurt Warner, or the Sultan of Brunei. I'm talking about, for instance, who do I want David Nelson to be? Follow me, and I will take you on a journey where you will create your future self.

Let's begin at the end . . . of your life.

The Eulogy Exercise

The Eulogy is intended to be a practical exercise that helps you define what you believe your ultimate objectives are on this planet, in this lifetime (if you believe in that sort of thing). While thinking about your own demise might seem to be kind of a downer at first, I have found that the Eulogy Exercise has always been a positive, fun experience in my workshops and seminars.

Step 1: Visualize your own funeral after your long life. Spare no expense; make it as simple or as grand as you like. Picture who is there and what the venue looks like. Yes, design your own funeral; this might be the only opportunity you get to do so.

Step 2: After some formalities, five people eulogize you: your spouse or partner, your child (even if you don't have one), a sibling or other relative, a co-worker and a member of your community. Picture each of them speaking about you. Hear their voices. Make a list of the qualities you would like them to say you had in those relationships. For example, what would you like your child to say about you as a parent? One thing I would like my child to say is that I gave him good guidance as a parent. In addition, make a list of the things that you personally would like to experience/accomplish for yourself.

At the end of this exercise, you should have a list of traits you want to be remembered for having.

Step 3: The next step is to determine what kind of behavior you would have to exhibit in order for someone to say X about you. In my example, I would determine what behaviors I would need to exhibit on a regular basis that would cause my son to conclude that I gave him good guidance.

- Perhaps I helped him separate his thoughts from his emotions.

- Perhaps I also helped him see things from a perspective different from his own.

- Perhaps I helped him think through tough decisions.

- Perhaps I always was focused on him when he was talking to me.

The idea here is to work backwards from the statement to

the kinds of behavior that support that statement.

Step 4: At your funeral, everyone will be talking about that one phrase that describes the way you lived your life. Your life's objective was abundantly clear to all. As you float around the room and listen in on various conversations, what do you want to hear? Do you want your family, friends and colleagues to say things like: "So-and-so knew more dirty jokes than anyone I've ever known!" Of course not. You want them to say, "So-and-so knew how to make and save money better than Howard Hughes." No? Then give it some thought. I'd recommend journaling about the topic.

Step 5: Once you have established how you want to be remembered, you have established what you want your life's objectives to be from now on. Write them down every day in your journal. Say them to yourself as you go to sleep. Wake up each morning with a picture in your mind of who you will be and how you will manifest that vision though specific behaviors.

Step 6: Knowing your destination is only the first piece of information you need in order to begin your journey. Before you plan your trip, you must also know where you are now. A simple analogy will describe this step. Think about what happens when you go to a shopping mall you've never been to. Let's say you want to find your favorite gadget store. You look it up on the directory, you find out it is at space #204 and then what happens? What else do you have to locate after you have found #204 on the map? That red arrow or dot that says: "You are here."

And you can find out where you are now by simply observing your behavior and taking responsibility for the choices you have made. After all, the choices you have made have played a big part in making you who you are today.

How do you want to be? It's a choice.

My experience tells me that the question "How do I want to be?" is the response to almost any situation I find myself in where I am making a choice. The way I see it, each choice I make is part of a larger picture of what I am telling myself, and the world outside of me, about who I really am.

In my seminars, when I begin my discussion about choices, I usually don't get any objection. But when I proceed to the precise definition of the word choice, I often get some resistance. *Each time you make a decision about how you are going to proceed in a situation, you are making a choice that tells the world a little something about who you are.* Sounds simple, right? But when the chips are down, some people suddenly forget that the position they are in is due largely to the decisions they have made. Suddenly, there are all kinds of forces and people and combinations thereof that are responsible for why they have found themselves in such a pickle.

When Lee bought her first house in the suburbs after living in the center of Chicago for most of her adult life, she was very excited about having a lawn and a garden of her own for the very first time. Unfortunately for her, amid the excitement about her new, plush greenery, she neglected to consider how time-consuming it was going to be to maintain it.

Lee developed an intense dislike for lawn mowing and shrub clipping. And she was angry that the previous owner didn't warn her about all that she would have to learn and do in order to keep the grounds attractive. Various plant foods; fertilize this, don't fertilize that; water this, but not too much and don't ever water that. It was all too much for her and she would complain to her friends: "No, I can't take that intensive yoga class this afternoon, I have to take care of my %^#&ing property! Boy did I make a mistake buying this place!"

While she was busy being angry with the previous owner and the exotic flowers, Lee failed to admit to the reality that she was the sole creator of her current state of emotion. Once she realized how much work it would take, she could have:

- Decided to replace the lawn with wood chips and get rid of the garden.
- Decided to hire someone to maintain the property.
- Decided to move if she couldn't afford or didn't want to allocate money toward paying someone to maintain the property.
- Decided to do the work herself and not complain, recalling that the grounds were the reason she chose the house.
- Decided to do the work herself and keep complaining.

Note the last suggestion. Doesn't it sound ridiculous? I think it does. Yet I'm sure everyone has made a decision similar to this. Although a variety of alternatives exist, we often choose to not alter the situation that is irking us, preferring to continue to complain about it. And that complaining is not into a vacuum; it tells the world a little bit about who we are. It tells the world that we would rather place blame than take responsibility and take action.

The next time you find yourself complaining, ask yourself what you have done to get yourself to that point, and what you can immediately do to get yourself out of that position (hence, that state of mind).

Every Choice Has Consequences

My personal belief is that complaining is not a productive use of time. It does not accomplish anything and it annoys surrounding people. If we want to minimize the amount of complaining we do, we could begin by accepting the various potential consequences of the choices we make.

We humans have a nasty habit of wanting to make choices and having the reality of those choices be different from what we already know to be true – remember the Home Depot example? This is where honesty is especially important. You are an expert at self-deception; we all are. Probably one of the most difficult yet beneficial things we could do to try to better ourselves is to stop lying to ourselves. It might sound harsh, but most of us have done it, and many of us have made a career of it. The fact is that we all realize that every choice has consequences, and we often know precisely what those consequences are. Nevertheless, we all have a habit of acting thoroughly surprised when those consequences (which we were aware of), actually occur.

One of my favorite examples of this occurs each day at airports around the world. I travel a lot for business and it has always amazed me that people are so shocked and incredulous when their flight has been delayed say, for mechanical reasons. After all, think of how many parts there are on a plane and how important it is that they are all functioning properly. It should not be surprising to anyone that sometimes a part breaks or malfunctions and a flight must be delayed.

Then there are the people who fly to Chicago in the winter and are stunned when their flight is delayed because of the weather. Need I say more?

Does that sound familiar?

If you are a chronic complainer, or a chronic-anything-negative (insert your nasty trait here), I've got some great news for you: It doesn't have to be that way.

You have learned to be who you are.

Much of your behavior was learned from your childhood. This is good news, because you can change many of the behaviors that you do not like. You learned to be a complainer (perhaps because it once served a function), and you can unlearn that behavior. You learned to be impatient, so you can learn to be patient. Here's how . . .

The Rules of Changing

I promised I would tell you what to do about those two big faults of yours. Here is the big secret of The Rules of Changing. Oddly enough, they begin with not trying to change. Instead, they involve something we were all masters at when we were children: pretending (i.e., make believe, or as I used to say as a child, "make pretend"). So if one of your faults is that you are impatient, I suggest pretending to be patient. Conjure up the image of a patient person you know. What do they do, how do they look, what bothers them and what doesn't phase them? How would they act/react in a situation that would cause *you* to be impatient? Picture yourself being that patient person. Now, pretend to be like that. Fake yourself out.

You cannot just change with the flick of a switch—you have to alter your behavior over time and learn a different way through repetition. So keep the image of your patient self in your mind, and summon it to consciousness whenever you feel the urge to be impatient.

I do not think pretending is easy, particularly at the beginning because you have to constantly remind yourself of what you should be doing. But the more you experience pretending, the faster the new, desired behavior will become a part of you. What was once pretend will become real.

Change and Your Eulogy

When you think about what you want people to say about you at your funeral, you are creating a model for your future self. The next step is to examine the list of characteristics your future self will have by then, and begin to plan your journey of transformation into that person. Some parts of your evolution will involve changing who you are now, and others will involve developing traits that you never had.

My only caveat is this: *All of your goals for who you want to be should be things you can control.* For instance, you cannot change the facts of the past. You can change your perception of them and your memory of them, but you cannot alter what has already occurred. You cannot control the actions, beliefs, or emotions of others. Influence, yes; control, no. Focus on you, how you behave today, and how you will choose to behave tomorrow.

The Fifth Key
Life Is Reasonable

Perhaps this childhood scenario sounds familiar . . .

You are at the bottom of the ninth inning of wiffle ball, bases are loaded and the score is tied. You want to stay outside but your mother says it's time to wash up for dinner. "NOW." "Why?" you scream. "Because I said so," she confidently retorts. You grab your things and stomp to the house, giving your mother the evil eye the entire time. You muster up the nerve to say "That's not fair," to which she immediately responds, "Who said life is fair?"

Your Mother was Right

In a perfect world, life would be fair. But that is completely irrelevant given the reality that the world we live in is not always fair. I am not going to say that you have no right, at any point in your life, to expect things to go your way. That would discourage you from thinking positively and using affirmations in your life.

But what I am going to say is that when something happens in your life that you do not like, fairness has nothing to do with it. The universe has not signed a contract with you guaranteeing a life of health and bliss. As the books say, bad things really do happen to good people. And they happen to bad people. And what's worse, really good things seem to happen sometimes to really bad people.

Depending on your belief system, you may believe that there is a plan for you and all of the good and bad things are on some cosmic blueprint. Let me make my belief clear and very simple: things you like and things you don't like are all part of being alive.

So how do we deal with this reality that life isn't "fair?" Well, maybe we need to start with investigating how the word "fair" is defined. "You got what you deserved" was a phrase I often heard as a child. Unfortunately, things often happen that have nothing to do with you, or anything you did. The problem comes in when we define "fair" as: Things should only be unpleasant when we did something "wrong" or "bad." Therefore, whenever anything unpleasant happens that has nothing to do with anything we did, we view it as being inherently unfair.

Yet, in our highly complex world, many things happen each day that are completely out of our control and have nothing to do with anything we have done. They are, however, often related to the choices we have made.

To continue with my earlier example, airplanes have millions of parts, and it is *reasonable* that periodically one of them will break. It is *reasonable* that there will be periodic weather delays in Chicago in the winter. And, if you choose to fly (and to fly through Chicago in the winter) it is *reasonable* that you may experience one or both of these realities. Is life fair? Well, I suppose that depends on your definition of "fair." Is life reasonable? Definitely! And usually in a predictable and consistent way. All we need to do is to become aware of it and accept it.

Free Will

Another part of my belief system, which is a vital part of all of the major religions I have studied, is that part of being a human on this planet is that you have *free will*. In other words, although your life may appear to have a direction of its own and you may at times feel like a pawn, it is precisely those times that you should remember that you always have choices. Unfortunately, when your perception is that things aren't going well for you, you are less likely to see the options you have.

Free Will and Choice

In the previous section I discussed the Eulogy Exercise. One of my objectives for that discussion was to explain the idea that much of our lives are the way they are because of the choices we have made. And we are in a position to make choices because our Creator has given us the ability to do so. That is free will.

Given the fact that we have the ability to make many choices in our lives, I'm sure you will agree that it would behoove us to make the best choices we can. But life has so many variables and that isn't always possible. All of us make what we like to call "bad choices" all of the time. My feeling is that the key to handling the bad choices begins with taking responsibility for them, and rectifying any problems you have created, rather than hiding or denying what you have done.

Don't expect anyone to rescue you from making a bad choice.

I have observed an ironic phenomenon of rescue-entitlement among people who have a history of making what they call "bad decisions." Their internal script goes something like this: *I will make choices and refuse to think of them as my choices if the outcome is negative. If the outcome is positive, however, it is because of me. But back to the negative stuff. If something negative occurs, I will be dismayed, and I will expect any and every person in my path to do whatever they can in order to immediately remedy the situation.*

I think back to the many flights that are delayed, and the many flight attendants who are screamed at by irate individuals. The rationale is in the order of: *I have an appointment to get to, and if this plane doesn't take off in the next 20 minutes, I am going to be late. Therefore, someone simply must do something to rectify the situation so I am not late again because of these darn unreliable, flippin' airlines.*

Let us examine this thinking. The problem is simple: All things in the universe have not been created in order to make your time on this planet more enjoyable. In other words, *you are not the Center Of the Universe.* I know, I know, you don't think you are. Neither do I.

However, there are times (particularly times when you want something) that you conveniently assume the role of Center Of the Universe. This manifests itself in your acting as if you are entitled to have all things go as you wish. Why? Because all things were created for you, personally. We all know that you, Y-O-U, don't really feel that way. But your C-O-U (Center of Universe) does.

C-O-U (Center of the Universe)

My advice to you is the same advice I give all of my clients, regarding *all* situations: When something goes "wrong" (a.k.a. not the way you wanted), remember that it is your COU who is upset. The moment you recall the COU, you will recall that at no point did you sign a contract with the universe guaranteeing that all things would go your way. Furthermore, when something goes amiss and the result is that your plans have changed, most of the time you personally had nothing to do with whatever went amiss. Repeat after me: *Sometimes the things that happen have nothing to do with me.*

In other words, except in rare instances, no one is out to get you. There is no conspiracy. You simply live in a time and place where there are a virtually infinite number of variables that affect what occurs in your life each day. Just about anything can happen. Remember what your mother said: "Who said life is fair?"

Possible Conclusion:
We have no control over what happens to us.

Ah, if that were only the truth. I would like to say that if something unpleasant occurs, it definitely had nothing to do with you. Unfortunately, I cannot. The reality is that we have *free will.* Recall that free will is probably the most important thing our Creator has given us. Think about it; we actually get to make lots of choices, each day, that dictate the direction of our lives.

For some people, however, free will is the enemy because they tend to make "bad decisions." And when they make "bad decisions," unpleasant consequences seem to be around the corner.

Before we go any further, I suggest rephrasing "bad decision/choice." Optimally, we make decisions after careful consideration of all alternatives. So if you make a choice and something unpleasant occurs, your choice was bad, right? Not necessarily.

For example, I finally decided to try a new restaurant that my friend, Tim, had been incessantly raving about. I sat at my table for a few minutes before I saw a waiter, my sea bass was okay, but not great, and my chocolate cake was not all that fresh. And for that, I paid twice as much as I do at my favorite café. Was my experience unpleasant? Yes. Did I make a bad choice by going to the restaurant? No. I made a great choice based on the information I had. And what's more, I learned a lesson about restaurant recommendations (i.e., they are personal – more on that later).

Choices are not intrinsically good or bad, they are just choices (with the obvious exception of purposely choosing to do something with the specific intent of doing harm – but then you would never do that!). Furthermore, whatever outcome results is just an outcome; it isn't good or bad either. Something—anything—becomes good or bad only because you perceive it to be. So if you make a choice and something unpleasant happens, I submit that you have given your perception of the outcome too much power.

In addition, you are giving *yourself* too much power. We do not know why all things occur. (For example, every restaurant has a bad day.) If something unpleasant occurs after you have made a choice, you do not always know for certain that you are the cause of the unpleasantness. Remember, there are myriad variables involved in most situations, and your decision is just one of them.

Who Else is Playing?

Given that there could be hundreds of variables related to any given situation you find yourself in, you could easily become discouraged. But that is a choice. On the flipside, you could realize that there are also lots of things that you can control, and most of them are conveniently located right inside you. You can control what you do, what you say and even what you think, as I have discussed.

And while you cannot control how others react to you, you can go a long way to managing their reactions by paying attention to how your choices seem to affect them. In other words, if you are concerned with how your life affects the lives of those around you, ask yourself "Who else is playing?" Who is around you and do they have a history of reacting in a certain way? If so, you could choose to change the usual course of events.

Grace had spent much of her 40 years resenting her virtually estranged father for not being communicative, warm, or involved in her life. Just prior to each holiday, she would call her father to try to arrange a meeting with him during the brief time she would be in the same state. Each time, he would seem enthused to hear from her, and he would make a tentative plan to meet with her. And each time she landed at the airport and called him, he would suddenly be unable to see her.

Grace didn't want to give up on her father because she only had one father, and in her mind, that was better than none. Each holiday, every family member felt a pall hanging over the holiday due to Grace's sadness and anger.

Grace tried many different ruses over the years to get her dad involved, but all were unsuccessful. She viewed the situation as "impossible," and she called herself a "failure" as a daughter. She thought she should be able to get her father to realize that their relationship was important and worth trying to repair.

I know several people with issues similar to Grace's. Unfortunately, the world is full of such scenarios that go on for lifetimes. While I understand the notion that family members are forever and that we should try to maintain them, I would suggest a different tack.

There is a way to maintain contact with her dad, but Grace should abandon the idea that she is ever going to have the kind of relationship she wants to have with him. There is a history with this particular relationship that is consistent. And though she is intellectually aware that she can *control* only her own behavior and try to manage others, her behavior contradicts that alleged awareness. *Grace is trying to change someone else and manage his reaction to her when she knows (intellectually) that is futile.* I'd bet that you see a bit of Grace in yourself. Perhaps now you see that this strategy is precisely the inverse of the correct way to handle a relationship.

Grace needs to change her strategy, and that change should begin with the way she talks about the situation. That talk (to others as well as to herself) will dictate how she views it, and it will probably ultimately be responsible for the outcome. Perhaps you too need to alter the way you speak and think about some aspects of your life.

Grace has called the situation "impossible" and viewed herself as a "failure" for not being able to get her father to see the light. Perhaps now it is a bit clearer to you why Grace has such a quandary. Grace has created her own mindset. Her father has always responded the same way to her, and trying to change him has not worked. At some point, Grace needs to accept that she does not have the power to make her father change.

After all these years, Grace's father has – for whatever reason(s) – shown that he either doesn't want to, or is unable to, maintain a close relationship with Grace. While I certainly understand Grace's disappointment with this, there comes a point in time when Grace's emotional state is no longer a result of her father's actions. Rather, it becomes a result of Grace's failure to accept her father's reality. Grace needs to take control of this situation by accepting her father as he is and, based on that, determine how she wishes to structure her future interaction with him.

Though she may decide that she wishes to continue to allocate time toward developing a relationship with her father, she will find that doing so will be less upsetting and less frustrating if she is able to change *her expectation about the results*. Grace is basing her success on how her father reacts, which is something she cannot control.

Instead, Grace needs to concentrate on whether she is conducting herself in a way she believes is correct. That is all that she can do. I would submit that far from failing, Grace has been successful. Despite her father's reaction, Grace has continued to be loving and supportive. She continues to maintain contact and that contact tells her father that she is there for him. And she has continued to do so long after many others would have given up.

In other words, she is conducting herself in a way she can be proud of. The fact that her father is not responding the way she would like him to– while disappointing to be sure – is not an indication that Grace has "failed." And it is essential that she not view it this way. Grace's criteria for judging herself needs to be her own actions – not her father's reactions.

On The Flip Side . . .

My friend Jack was given up by his birth mother at an early age. Jack is now in his late twenties and has recently started searching for his birth mother and any other biological family members. After spending considerable time and resources on the Internet, with local officials, and searching through records and databases, Jack found out that he had a very large biological family – some of whom lived within miles of his home!

While the location of his birth mother still eluded him, Jack was ecstatic about finding other family members and he set out to meet every member of his "real" family that he could. Over the next few weeks, Jack reported back to me each time he met someone new in his family. He noted that they had similar features and spoke in a similar way and with many of the same mannerisms, etc. Jack loved this whole process but was frustrated by the missing piece to the puzzle—he was still not able to locate his mother.

Utilizing information from his various family members – coupled with his continuing investigative efforts – Jack eventually tracked down an address for his birth mother. He was excited and nervous when he made the first call to her. We spoke shortly after that and Jack shared with me his plans of going to California to finally meet his birth mother. He simply couldn't wait and planned his trip for that very weekend! We agreed to meet for lunch the day after he returned.

I had expected to see a beaming Jack at lunch that day, but instead was greeted by a sullen and sad Jack. Obviously concerned, I asked him what happened on his trip.

> *Jack: "It was weird, Dave. I was all set for an exciting family reunion – but when I arrived my mother was not at all what I had hoped. She was very emotionally unstable, her house was filthy and she appeared to be unhappy in her current marriage. She was manipulative and she blamed others for what happened to her in her life. She seemed to care little about what had happened in my life and was completely focused on herself! It was a real bummer. I'm almost sorry now that I pursued this whole "family" thing."*

Jack and I chatted for a while that day. I told him that while I certainly understood his disappointment, not all of his experiences with his newly found family were like the one with his mother. In fact, of the 10 or 12 relatives he found, only his time with his birth mother had been unpleasant; the rest had been warm, loving and accepting. While Jack agreed with this, it took him some time to realize that he needed to stop focusing on how his mother wasn't what he wanted her to be, and to begin focusing on all of the other relatives who were becoming a positive part of his life. Jack's mother is how she is – he cannot control that.

It's easy in life to get focused on things that are not how we want them to be. Focusing on all that is right – and letting go of the things/people you can't control – is essential to taking control of your own life and emotional state.

The Sixth Key

Draw the Right Picture

We tend to think that reality is a constant and universal thing. I would submit, however, that reality—like beauty—is in the eye of the beholder. If you accept that reality is a combination of the things that happen to you and your reaction to them, it would follow then that each of us has a different reality. Each of our realities is unique to us, yet shared by all with whom we come into contact, because our realities affect our choices.

While you are not always able to control what happens in your life, you are always able to control *the way you think about* what happens to you. You create your personal reality with the way you talk to yourself and others: with the words and phrases you use every day.

Out of the mouths of babes . . . . or muppets

I'm sure you know, or have heard of, Oscar the Grouch from Sesame Street. If you recall, or if you have small children, you know that Oscar the Grouch is a muppet (but don't say that to his face) who lives in a garbage can. Grouchland, in the movie *Elmo in Grouchland* is, dare I say, a garbage dump. But those who live in Grouchland see it as a beautiful kingdom. In fact, the Queen of Trash, played by singer/actress/former Miss America Vanessa L. Williams, sings a song with the following chorus, joined, of course, by scores of singing bits of garbage. It goes something like this . . .

Take a look around and tell me you don't see
just a worthless pile of garbage and debris
I see a kingdom, shining bright
If you try you can see it too

You find the beauty if you look at something right . . .
In life, it's all about your point of view.

Relanguaging

A couple of decades ago it was possible to argue that words are just words. Only fringe types would have argued that the words we use profoundly affect who we are and what happens to us. However, now that Tony Robbins is practically a household name and Oprah Winfrey talks about affirmations to an audience of millions each day, the message is clear: the words you use shape your life.

Relanguaging, as of this writing, is not a word that is in the dictionary. However, due to its popularity in the self-improvement world, I have no doubt that it will be adopted by the mainstream in no time. Allow me to explain what relanguaging means.

The word language is ordinarily used as a noun. Recall from your grammar school days that nouns are people, places and things. Re- is a prefix that precedes verbs (action words), and means "to do again" (e.g., rewrite). So ordinarily, re- would not precede the word *language*. Here, however, *language* is being used as a verb. The verb that it is most similar to is the verb to speak. But to language is more than just to speak. *Languaging* involves what is going on in your mind as you choose the words and phrases you say to yourself and to others. Languaging, therefore, assumes you are aware of the potential impact of words, and you will choose carefully. It is about intention.

*Re*languaging, then, means that you are examining what you have said and the impact it had (on you and your audience), and you have opted to revise your original expression in favor of a more productive one. You relanguage because you want to optimize your words.

If, upon examination, you discover that the words you are using do not accurately express your intentions or beliefs or in some cases, even your reality, you ought to change them. I will use this section to present you with some of the most common ways we tend to misspeak and miscommunicate. Misspeaking usually originates in not taking ample time to think before you speak. Part of the nature of misspeaking is typically that you don't know you are doing it. And it is most often a result of traits you have learned over a long period of time. Mis*communication*, however, comes from thinking you are sending one message, but you are really sending a different one. The result is unclear or inadequate communication.

Many people fly through the following common verbal crimes and misdemeanors, thinking they do not apply to them (although they usually know a lot of perpetrators). I suggest you take your time reading the explanations and the stories, and reflect upon your own life and consider the possibility that you too just might have something in common with the people in the stories.

David's Top Five Verbal Crimes and Misdemeanors

#5 Bad vs. Unpleasant

Things have happened in your life that have been unpleasant experiences for you. But verbal crime #5 is calling those things "bad." And when "bad" things happen, it is customary to think that somehow you have been wronged ("poor you"). Sound familiar? I contend that lots of unpleasant situations and experiences will come your way, but to call them "bad" is a misnomer.

Part of life on this planet is the experience of unpleasantness, and to start labeling all of those experiences "bad" is to introduce an element of negativity into your life that is unnecessary and can even be detrimental. Remember that if you say "love" to yourself over and over again you are likely to begin to feel "love." What do you think will happen if you say "bad" over and over again?

To make matters more realistic, sometimes you must make a choice between something unpleasant and something *more* unpleasant. No one looks forward to these kinds of decisions, but that doesn't mean that anything "bad" is involved. It also doesn't mean you did anything wrong by being in the position where you had to choose between unpleasant options.

Haven't you ever had an unpleasant experience that took you someplace good? We all have. So we should stop attaching negativity to all experiences that are not what we expected. We have to get out of the mindset that if it wasn't in our plan, it must have been wrong.

Estelle was looking for an inexpensive place to live and stumbled upon her dream house—one that had every requirement she had. This was a small miracle, as her requirements were that the house: was on the shore, had a lap pool, had a rock garden, had a huge kitchen with slate floors, and had a cathedral ceiling.

The house she found had another added bonus: it was rent-free because the owner needed someone to take care of it for two years while he was overseas. Estelle sold her condo, put her belongings in storage and packed her bags. The next day, the homeowner's overseas plans fell through and the deal was off. Estelle was devastated—and homeless.

The man knew many property owners in town and said he would try to find her a place. He did. It was an apartment in an old building on the other side of town, over a mile from the shore, where Estelle could rent month-to-month until she found a better place. She was miserable and her new place was in need of some work. After several days of wallowing, she decided to clean the apartment, do some minor decorating and make the best of it.

One of her home improvements was a small cement sculpture that she couldn't carry by herself. She decided to recruit someone from the building. A moment later, a man just back from his daily run approached the apart-

ment on the floor below her. He was already sweaty, and he looked strong, so she thought he wouldn't mind helping. Within a year they were married, and they have remained happy together for over a decade.

Estelle's story illustrates several important lessons about "bad" experiences as well as "bad" decision-making. At one point, her initial decision to take the offer of the dream house appeared to be a "bad" one (i.e., when she found out the deal was off and she didn't have a Plan B). And it certainly led to some unpleasantness. But when you fast-forward to the end of the story, you know that she met her husband at her new home. And she wouldn't have moved into that new home if she hadn't been practically forced to do so because of her unpleasant circumstances.

So did anything *bad* really happen? Sure, Estelle was inconvenienced and had to spend some money to make her new apartment a place she would like to live in. But is that really "bad?" After all, once she was through wallowing, she was able to make her new apartment into a home that she enjoyed. And then the icing on the proverbial cake was meeting her husband! Did getting there involve some unpleasantness? Sure it did! Did that unpleasantness therefore make the decision "bad" or "wrong"? Absolutely not! Quit assuming that just because something is unpleasant that it's bad. Make the best of what comes your way and see where it takes you!

#4 Must/Gotta/Have to

These are three words/phrases that are so over used that in the rare instances that they are actually appropriate, they do not have the impact they should have.

- I have to mow the lawn.
- I gotta go grocery shopping
- I must get out of bed and get ready for work.

It has been my experience that there are very few things we truly *must* have in order to maintain our human existence on this planet. I have yet to come up with more than four: air, water, food and shelter. Some people think my list is incomplete; they'd like to add things like love, cell phones, Internet access, chocolate, etc.

But I am not talking here about what you find pleasurable or what makes doing your business easier; I am talking about what do you *need* in order to stay alive – what you *must* have to survive. Anything beyond those four are things you are *choosing* to have, probably to make your live easier or happier. Since all we really *need* is air, water, food and shelter, we will have more control over our lives when we can change our usage of the terms must, gotta and have to.

For example, my neighbor Joe was outside mowing his yard one day – sweaty and not looking like he was having much fun. As he got over to my side of his yard, I yelled out that he didn't look like he was having a very good time. He turned the mower off, wiped his brow and headed over to the fence, saying, "Man, I hate having to mow this yard. I only have one day off this week and here I am out here sweatin' my behind off. This stinks!" With that said, he restarted the mower and got back to the task at hand.

Now, you may know people who have said something similar – perhaps about cleaning, laundry, driving in traffic, any number of things. You may have even felt this way yourself at times.

So what are our learning opportunities here? Well, let's look at the words Joe used…"I hate *having to* mow this yard." By using the words *having to* Joe is creating a picture in his own mind – a mental state of being *forced* to do something. It's as if something or someone other than Joe is saying to him: "You *have* to do this." Psychologically, whenever we are forced to do something two things happen:

1. We are not able to enjoy, or even put up with, the activity. Instead, we begin to "hate" it. This, of course, means that the time we spend doing it is lost.

2. We will eventually begin to resent the *source* of the force. This will most likely not be a conscious thought on our part. Rather, it will become one of the sub-surface emotional thoughts that manifest itself (usually in conjunction with others of similar ilk, but from different sources) in a sharp word or phrase, a short temper, greater focus on self, a decrease in being Actively Considerate, etc.

Once again, the real issue here has to do with *choices*. What may seem like a simple misuse of words is actually an implicit refusal to take responsibility for your choices. Each day, thousands of times if not more, you make decisions. You don't have to wake up early to go to work, you choose to. You choose to then shower before you go to work and you choose not to speed (too much) on the way. You choose to leave home early enough to allow for some rush hour traffic, and you choose to obey traffic laws. You choose to do your job all day and then return home to fulfill your role with your family.

Hopefully, you do these things because you believe the benefits you receive from them are worth the inherent tradeoffs that come with doing them. Knowing these benefits and tradeoffs and taking the conscious responsibility for the decisions and choices you make are essential steps to taking control of your life.

The only thing you can do when you need to make a choice that will impact your life, is to ask yourself:

1. What are the positive and negative potential outcomes?

2. Does receiving the potential positives outweigh putting up with the negative outcomes, should they occur?

If the answer to this question is "yes, I am willing to accept the potential downsides" – then proceed. But if it is "no" then do not proceed! Furthermore, do not deceive yourself by factoring in probability. Too often we will say things like, "Well, there's such a slight chance that will happen that I'm not even going to worry about it." While I would agree that low probability outcomes might not be worth "worrying" about, they certainly should not be dismissed as not being possible. If it is a possibility, then you must at least have determined that you are willing to accept that outcome should it occur. Not doing so misleads you and sets you up for anger and frustration.

Every decision has consequences and possible outcomes. To have true control over your life, you must accept that it is *your* responsibility to think through the consequences of your decisions. You must decide what it is you want vis-à-vis what you are willing to accept should things not turn out as desired. To be aware of all the possible outcomes of a decision you make, and to make that decision and experience (as is often the case in life) one of the unpleasant outcomes inherent in that decision, *and to then complain about it*—is, quite frankly, a waste of time and energy.

Is The Force Really With You?

When you think or say that you *must* do something, it's as if you think that there is some force that is giving you no choice but to do that thing. When you use the language of must/gotta/have to, you are using the language of a victim, of someone who has no control over his or her life. In reality, though, how often is that the case? How often is there an outside force making you do something against your will?

Let's go back to my neighbor, Joe. Does Joe really *have* to mow his yard? Of course not! Joe has a variety of choices other than mowing the yard himself. As Joe made his next pass by me, I decided to ask him whether he had considered his options.

> *David: "Hey Joe, you really seem to dislike moving the yard, have you considered hiring someone to do it for you?"*
>
> *Joe: "Yeah, but it would cost me over $100 a month and that's money I can put toward the kids' college – every bit helps."*
>
> *David: "Good point. Well, then how about just pulling up the grass, putting in a big deck and then mulching the rest?"*
>
> *Joe: "That would certainly eliminate the mowing! But I enjoy having a yard – barbequing and such – and it's a good play space for the kids."*
>
> *David: "Very true. I suppose you could sell the place and move to a big condo; there they maintain the grounds for you."*
>
> *Joe: "Nah – I like havin' my own space – it's a reminder to me that I have achieved a certain level of financial success. And to be honest, I do enjoy how good it looks after I'm finished – if only it would stay that way!"*
>
> *David: "Hmmm. Well, it sounds to me that based on the various choices you have, you have chosen to mow the yard. In fact, by mowing the yard yourself, you accomplish several things that are important to you: You have a sense of pride in your home ownership, you enjoy how your yard looks when you finish, and you feel a sense of accomplishment. And to boot, you are able to contribute more toward the educational expenses of your kids! I'm sure that brings you a great sense of security. Then there's the bonus that your family is able to have a safe*

play place and you enjoy the time you can spend here barbequing. Given all those benefits – compared to the time and energy spent mowing the yard – it seems to me that you made a pretty good choice in deciding to have a yard in the first place, and then to maintain it yourself."

Joe: "Gee, I never looked at it like that, but I guess you're right! I suppose I am choosing to do this to get certain benefits. But it's still an effort."

David: "I hear you there; most decisions we make have two sides. But I think that if you can focus on the benefits you are getting by making this choice, it will make the task less daunting. You might also look for some ways to make the task more pleasant. Wear some headphones and listen to that music you like that your wife hates or most anything that would make the time and task more enjoyable.

But I'll tell you this much, Joe: I've learned over time that when I make a choice and then spend time and energy complaining about it, the only thing I'm accomplishing is making that time unpleasant for myself. I always have a choice – I just have to remember to focus on the benefits I'm receiving from my choices – and accept the inherent responsibilities that go along with them – doing what I can to make the experience as pleasant as possible."

Joe: "Good points, Dave. I'm going to head in right now and get that Walkman – and the Led Zeppelin tape Mary hates– and go finish up the yard. Thanks!"

Even when it's not fun – it's still your choice.

The important lesson here is that you are in charge of the choices we make. All choices have tradeoffs – and when making decisions you need to weigh the benefits and responsibilities and then decide if the responsibilities you assume with the decision are worth the benefits you will receive. If they are – then do it. If they aren't, then don't. As I said earlier, to make a choice and then spend time and energy complaining about it only serves to decrease the quality of your life and make you a victim.

#3 Stating your opinion as fact

Last summer I was talking to my old friend, Karen, who off-handedly asked:

> *Karen: "Hey David, did you see the new Mission Impossible movie?"*
>
> *David: "No."*
>
> *Karen: "Oh, you've got to see it; it is such a fantastic movie!"*

Brief exchanges like this happen all of the time. Let's examine it. What I'd like to address about Karen's opinion, is that she makes no mention of it being her opinion. She uses the word "is," which is known as a verb of being. She is, in effect, saying that the inherent nature of the movie is that it is fantastic. Meanwhile, we both know she is talking about her opinion. I personally know lots of people who saw the movie and didn't like it, so clearly it is not inherently fantastic.

If it is your opinion that, for example, salmon tastes best when it is grilled, say "I like salmon when it is grilled," or "To me, grilled salmon tastes much better than poached salmon." I take note when someone I am speaking with takes the energy to preface their opinions with a comment that what they are going to say is a subjective matter.

A fact is. Opinions vary. So, when opinions are stated as facts, and those facts (which are really opinions) are in conflict, then one person must be wrong and another right. After all, two opposing "facts" cannot exist. Inevitably, the person who is "right" is perceived to be the winner while the person who is "wrong" is perceived to be the loser. And because none of us wants to be considered the loser, we try to win – through debate, argument and sometimes anger and fist-fights.

Much of this can be avoided by simply making sure that we state our opinions and beliefs as such – as things that are personal to us. And we should do this regardless of how many others share our opinions or beliefs. The prevalence of a belief or opinion does not make either a fact. One of the founding principals of our society is freedom of belief. When anyone's group begins to posture that its beliefs are fact and thus should apply to everyone – then that basic freedom of belief is taken away for everyone. If you want freedom of belief then you must be willing to give it (see The Eighth Key: Give What You Want to Get).

Part of what I am intending to do in this book, is to help you increase your awareness of the language you use and what it really means. Although each of these forays into language may seem insignificant standing alone, when you put them all together, they point to one thing: Taking control of your life – and letting others be in control of theirs.

Movies. Salmon. Death.

Movies and salmon are just the tip of the iceberg. What do they have to do with death? Well, just like a movie is not inherently bad or good, and grilled salmon is inherently no better than poached salmon, death is neither inherently good nor bad. In fact, there are very few things that are actually good or bad; it is our involvement that determines the emotional response of goodness or badness of something to us.

> *Most of Anna's 85 years were full of adventure and happiness. However the last few years brought many illnesses and an incapacitating fall that left her in a wheelchair. Unable to travel the way she was accustomed to, and*

unable to do many simple things for herself, she became depressed. One evening, she had a stroke while she was sleeping and had to be hospitalized. Her children and grandchildren visited her every day during her last week, and their behavior was indicative of their feelings about her impending death.

Anna's grandchildren brought her pictures, music and gifts to remind her of her long and happy life and to let her know how cherished she was. Their visits were spent re-telling old family stories, joking around and kissing and caressing their dying matriarch. They reminded her that she would soon be with her beloved husband, and with God.

Anna's children, on the other hand, who were in their fifties, had a much different approach. They reprimanded their own children for "horsing around" and called their behavior disrespectful. Their visits were spent mostly in silence, with an occasional prayer said aloud. Whenever they spoke with Anna's doctors, they asked if there was any way they could lengthen her life. They pursued every avenue.

Anna soon passed away and her children were devastated. Her grandchildren were sad, because they were going to miss Anna. But they were also happy for her, because the frustration of living in a body that didn't work had ended.

Was Anna's death good or bad?
That depends on whom you ask.

Stating your opinions as opinions is especially important if you have children because it teaches them that life is very much a matter of perspective. As children age and develop cognitively, they begin to be able to understand that things aren't as black and white, or good and bad, as they previously thought.

#2 Using the Word "Not"

If I had to change one thing about you (which we all know is futile, as you will change only when you're darn ready), it would be to get you to cease using the word not, particularly when you are talking to yourself. Why? Because there are better, more productive ways of phrasing your thoughts. In fact, the word "not" practically sets you up to produce contradictory results. Let me explain . . .

The subconscious is unable to process the word "not." Remember when you were a child and you were standing behind a red velvet rope waiting in line. Maybe you were at a museum, maybe you were going to see a movie, maybe you were at the airport. When your parents told you not to sneak under the rope (something parents invariably do), what was the first thing you thought of doing? The moment you tell someone not to do something, you have introduced the suggestion of doing whatever the unwanted behavior is. If, on the other hand, you tell them what you do want, that's all they have to think about: *Please stay on this side of the rope.*

This is a particularly helpful concept when you think about all of the ways you try to alter your own behavior by telling yourself what not to do. The next time you are about to tell yourself that you won't (insert the behavior you would like to extinguish), tell yourself to do the opposite, instead. After all, what you are really seeking is positive behavior, anyway, so why not ask for it?

A neighbor of mine just moved to Manhattan. When he was my neighbor, he lived in the suburbs in a house with a large garage. He parked his car in the garage. Not remarkable, right? Well, moving to the city has made it necessary for him to perfect his parallel-parking skills. If you've ever been to Manhattan, I'm sure you'll agree that each street holds more than its fair share of cars.

Each day for the first month at his new home, my neighbor hit one or both of the cars he was trying to park between. He did the same thing when exiting a parking

> *space. He had been driving for 20 years and this was very frustrating for him. He had heard all about "mind over matter" and he decided he was going to convince himself not to hit the cars. Each day, he repeated: "I will not hit those cars today." What do you think happened?*
>
> *I congratulated him for his line of thinking, and suggested a minor alteration. If he insisted on using some kind of mantra while parking, he should say something like: "I am a skilled parallel-parker and getting in and out of any space is easy for me." He thought that was "stupid" and "too long," but since his strategy wasn't working, he learned his new mantra.*
>
> *As you probably have guessed, his new mantra worked. The only remaining issue was that he claimed that he stopped hitting the cars because all of his practice had made him better. His newfound ease with parallel parking just happened to coincide with his relanguaging, he insisted. And that's fine with me.*

While this may seem to be simply a matter of semantics, there is more going on psychologically. When you speak to yourself, you are drawing a picture in your mind of what is. If you say, for instance, "it is really hot and humid out today" – then most likely the weather will feel particularly hot and humid, as you have drawn a picture in your mind of what to expect. If you say: "It just drives me crazy when I have to wait in a long line at the grocery store" – then most likely you will be crazed when you next wait in a long line in a grocery store. You have told your mind what behavior to exhibit when a particular situation occurs.

Your mind – while it may not seem like this at times – is a relatively obedient servant. The mind listens to what we tell it, draws a picture of the behavior we are referring to, and then goes about creating that behavior when called upon. In order to achieve more desired behavior, we just need to learn how to better teach our mind how to serve us.

When we attempt to change behavior, we often speak to ourselves in terms of what we won't do/be.

- I *will not* be impatient when faced with a long line at the store.
- I *will not* get upset when the kids whine about their bedtime.
- I *won't* hit the golf ball into the water on the next hole.

And so on and so on. Here's the problem: The mind cannot draw a behavioral picture of us *not* doing something.

The mind is only able to key in on the active words it hears. Let's take the golf example. What picture is your mind supposed to draw of your ball *not* going in the water? Where is it supposed to place the ball? In the sand trap? Up a tree? In the rough? There's no way to know. So, unable to determine what behavior it is you want, your mind pulls from your thoughts the active words it hears. I - Hit – Ball – Into – Water.

If you say "I will not get upset when the kids whine about their bedtime" – well what *will* you be doing? Getting angry? Tearful? Jovial? Patient? The mind is crying out: *Tell me what behavior you desire and I will create it for you – but I can't create you NOT being something*! So, again, it will pull from the active words you are telling it – I – Get – Upset – When – Kids – Whine.

So, when you are talking, either to yourself or to someone else, about what you want to achieve, keep your words focused on just that: what you want to achieve. Give your mind the words that describe the behavior you want to exhibit. If you wish to establish a new behavior, talk about the new behavior as if it has already begun ("I am a skilled parallel parker," rather than "I won't hit those cars anymore"). If you speak about anything as if it will occur someday in the future, it will always be out of reach. Speak in the present, and use positive language. Put your mind to work *for* you.

#1 "You make me feel . . . "

The next time these four words leave your mouth, think for a moment about what you are really saying. The message is clear: "You are so powerful, and I, on the other hand, am so weak, and so vulnerable to your suggestion that I simply must feel XX (e.g., angry, sad, guilty) and I have absolutely no choice but to feel XX (angry, sad, guilty), as you have thus commanded."

Now, you might be thinking that my explanation is a bit extreme. But when someone is *making* you do something, they are forcing you to do it. Implied in those words are that you have no choice. But that's a cop out. The reality is that you always have a choice.

The Seventh Key

Before You React, Consider Intent

I have examined what you say, and now it's time to examine what you do, and what that tells the world about who you are. When you look at your list of things you would like people to say about you at your funeral, how do they compare to how you are received right now? Are you the person you want to be? Are all of your actions consistent with your thoughts? Do you always do what you intend to do? My guess is that your answer is: sometimes yes, sometimes no. And if you sometimes do things that aren't received well or you sometimes *don't do anything* and are nevertheless not received well, remember one thing: You are not alone.

How considerate you appear to be in your relationships says a lot about how much you value those relationships. But if you do not appear to be considerate, that doesn't mean you *necessarily* don't care about a relationship. I like to think of behavior as Actively Inconsiderate, Passively Inconsiderate, Actively Considerate, or Actively Considerate—With Strings Attached. Read on and see if you find yourself anywhere in the following descriptions.

Actively Inconsiderate

When someone is behaving in an Actively Inconsiderate manner, they are *purposely* choosing an activity that is specifically designed to irritate, annoy, bother, or harm someone else.

Passively Inconsiderate

When someone is behaving in a Passively Inconsiderate manner, they usually have no idea that they are making other people angry or frustrated. The root of their problem is often that they are not considering the feelings or desires of others when they make their decisions. They are not malicious and they are not out to get you or anyone else. Most people who are labeled inconsiderate are Passively Inconsiderate.

The problem is that when someone is being inconsiderate, or is doing something we do not like or have deemed wrong, we act as though they are doing it with the intention of being irritating: that they are being Actively Inconsiderate. Moreover, we usually think they are trying to irritate us personally. In reality, though, there are very few people who spend their time and energy *purposely* doing things designed specifically to anger, bother, upset or harm others. That's why it is so important to consider intent prior to deciding how to we are going to react to the behavior of others. Here's an everyday example that you may relate to.

> *My friend Alex had picked me up at the airport one day as a favor. As we were nearing my house, a car pulled into our lane from a convenience store, making it necessary for Alex to brake quite a bit in order to slow down enough to avoid hitting the back end of that car. This wasn't a squealing tires kind of braking – just a hard brake. Alex's reaction to this was one I've seen often, and used to experience myself.*
>
> *Alex: (with the weight of his entire upper body on the horn): "Can you believe that guy? What a friggin' jerk- pulling out like that in front of me. What the hell is wrong with that guy?"*

Alex's reaction to this situation was quite visceral. As you can imagine, I toned down some of his actual descriptive words for the other driver. Alex continued on about the evil driver for a few minutes, and even broadened his commentary to include the general state of rudeness of people (himself excluded, of course) and how it seems that there are jerks everywhere. For those few precious minutes of his life (and all the minutes are precious – which is why we are working on ways to make each one of them as enjoyable as possible), Alex made himself angry, upset and generally miserable. I wanted to see if I could help Alex take control when things like this happened in the future.

David: "You know, Alex, I hate to admit this to you, but I've done that as well – several times in fact."

Alex: "What do you mean 'I've done that as well' – what have you done?"

David: That - I've pulled out of a parking lot before in front of someone and they had to put on the brakes real fast. I mean, not like on purpose or anything – I either just didn't see the person- perhaps I was distracted, or misjudged the speed they were driving, or misjudged the distance they were from me."

Alex: (laughing) "Well hell, I have too. In fact, it happened to me yesterday. I was turning onto 22nd and this guy was coming down the street – and he appeared to be pretty far away – but when I turned it seemed he was almost right behind me! I guess I misjudged how fast he was going. And man, was he peeved – laid right down on his horn. And I was like – geez – cut me some slack here buddy – sorry!"

David: "And did he cut you some slack?"

Alex: "No way - I could hear him yelling with the windows up!"

David: "That seems a bit unfair – I mean – it wasn't

like you saw him, knew how fast he was going and decided to turn in front of him just to irritate him."

Alex: "You got that right. But you know people never stop to think that maybe what you did was just an innocent mistake. They just get all crazed and act as if you were out to get them."

David: "Yeah – seems kind of like a huge waste of energy, huh? It would be great if people would cut everybody else some slack. I mean, rather than automatically assuming someone is being Actively Inconsiderate, we could instead choose to believe that the person made a simple mistake and just let it go. That would save a lot of negative energy on both parties' parts, don't you think?"

Alex: "Uh, yeah, it would. You know Dave, I hate it when you do this."

When you face situations like this – remember – it's not all about you. We all make mistakes/misjudgments in our everyday living. Just as you want others to forgive and be patient with yours, you should do so with them. In most cases, the perceived misdeed is innocent. Assume it is so and react accordingly. To do otherwise wastes time, energy and a part of your life.

Actively Considerate

People who behave in an Actively Considerate manner think about what others want and don't want, and then factor those needs and preferences into their behavior. These are the people who are likely to put the needs of others before their own.

Actively Considerate—With Strings Attached

To the untrained eye, these people appear to be just plain Actively Considerate. But upon closer inspection, although they do make choices that factor in what you need and want, they will remind you that they have done so. These are the people who do kind, generous things, but try to lay a guilt trip on you.

The strings that are attached are often strings of recognition. These people need to be acknowledged and need to feel appreciated for what they think is their selflessness. Unfortunately, this often detracts from the goodness of their behavior, as many recipients of their considerate behavior often feel like they are expected to return the favor.

Another potential string attached to the ostensibly selfless behavior of this type of person, is the *quid pro quo* (meaning, this for that). This is where the seemingly Actively Considerate person tells you exactly what you should do to fairly acknowledge their behavior. This is called manipulation, and leaves you feeling used.

A client of mine heard me talk about Actively Considerate behavior, and he realized that much of his behavior fell into the Passively Inconsiderate category. This was particularly true with his relationship with his wife, and he very much wanted to change. I'll call him Josh. Please eavesdrop on our conversation . . .

> *Josh: "David, I've got this great idea to kick off my metamorphosis into an Actively Considerate person. I am going to surprise my wife with a vacation to the Caribbean Islands. She's always wanted to go there and it'll make her so happy that I thought of it all by myself. I'm even going to make all of the arrangements. We'll spend a whole week together—just the two of us—just like before we got married and had the kids. It'll be like a second honeymoon."*
>
> *David: "That's a great concept, Josh. As long as your intention is to do something that'll make her really*

happy, why not let her pick the vacation spot?"

Josh: "Well, I could do that, but what if she doesn't pick a place that has golf?"

David: "I have seen lots of websites, and even some books, dedicated to golf vacations. If she likes golf so much, you could help her do the research. I'm sure she'd really appreciate that!"

Josh: "She doesn't play golf."

David: " Oh. Then . . . the golf is for . . . for you?"

Josh: "Well, yeah, I mean, what am I going to do for a week on some island in the middle of nowhere?"

David: "Josh, perhaps we should review what being Actively Considerate is all about. I applaud you for your intention to work on becoming more considerate. Remember, though, that a big part of such behavior is doing things that will make the other person happy. If you give your wife the choice of where to go, I bet she will gladly choose a place that has golf, for two reasons:

1. Because she doesn't have to. If you make it a requirement, she will rightfully question whether the vacation is really for her. If she feels like she is being manipulated, you probably won't end up going anywhere.

2. Because she is an Actively Considerate person already. She will always make choices with your needs and desires in mind."

Josh: "Okay, I get it, she gets to choose. But I hope she remembers that I let her choose the next time we go on vacation."

David: "I understand that you want to feel appreciated, Josh, and I don't think you should worry too much about it. Another part of being Actively Considerate is not requiring a payback for all of your good deeds and not keeping a scorecard. This isn't about doing something nice with the expectation that the deed will be not only acknowledged, but also repaid. You've still got strings attached to your kindness.

True giving is about doing something nice, something that you might not even enjoy doing, without the anticipation of being rewarded. In fact, sometimes the deed will go completely unrecognized."

Josh: "This is going to be tough to get used to. If there's anything I know about myself, it's that I need to be acknowledged."

David: "That's by no means a horrible trait, Josh, and I think we all have some of it. And I think that over time you'll get to the point where you realize that the recognition that counts the most is your own recognition. Eventually, you will do things and act ways simply for the pleasure of knowing that you are an Actively Considerate person. You will even get extreme feelings of accomplishment by not feeling the need to have anyone else know. But that is a long-term goal that takes time.

In the meantime, why not tell your wife that you are trying to be more Actively Considerate, and that during your transition you need her support in order to sustain that behavior? I'm sure that she'll be ecstatic that you have realized that you need to do some work. And she'll be doubly happy that you have a plan and you know you need clear signs of appreciation."

Discontent Breeds Change

Josh gradually evolved into a genuinely considerate person. He began his journey because he realized he was not happy with the way he was behaving. His wife had been unhappy for some time, but it took a while for him to grasp her unhappiness and admit to his contribution to her discontent.

Josh's case was not uncommon. When you are the party who is not content, you tend to be quicker to seek to alter whatever is responsible for your discontent. The most difficult part of this process is taking responsibility for your own unhappiness, and not blaming others. Remember, the direction you go in is your choice.

Are you content?

If you are not content, you know that you ought to do something to change your status. However, some people are content with who they are, yet others have a different opinion of them. In order to determine how others view you, you must ask them.

Ask them? How?

If you and those around you would not classify you as *Actively Considerate*, you have some work to do. In order to ascertain if this is the case, I suggest you make a list of the half dozen people whom you are closest to. From that list, pick three people who are the most sensitive and respectful, and who will not mock you when you ask them to help you better yourself.

You should read the definitions of the various levels of considerate behavior to your chosen three and ask them to talk to you about the way you appear to treat them and others. Because this is a delicate conversation, it is most successful when it is done at a time and place when neither of you is especially distracted, angry, or in a hurry. There is a time and place for everything, so choose yours wisely.

I recommend taping these conversations with a micro cassette recorder. Why? Because the moment you hear something you do not want to hear, you are likely to either not hear anything else thereafter, or misinterpret/mishear what the other person is saying. When you listen to the tape a couple of days later, I wager that what you hear then will be different from what you thought you initially heard. We are all human and we all do this; don't be too hard on yourself if this process isn't as uplifting as you thought it might be.

In addition, while you are conversing with your chosen three, try not to be defensive or respond to what your friends say, even with explanations for your behavior. This is an information-seeking mission, not an attack and defense.

If you ask for productive input, and you react as if your friends are attacking you, you are likely to end up in an argument. In order to decrease the probability that you actually do get verbally attacked, simply say: "I respect your opinion and I value our relationship. I am allowing myself to be vulnerable to you by asking for your help. Please respect that by providing me with examples or other information that addresses my question. Address my specific actions and avoid making judgments about them." Ask them to use phrases like – "when you do . . . I feel like . . ." rather than "you can really be a jerk when you . . . " If that doesn't work, start the process again with a different person.

Do Unto Others

Just as you would want others to consider what you intended to do and not rush to judgment based on what you have done, you should give them the same courtesy.

If someone does something you do not appreciate, before you label their behavior as bad or inconsiderate, or worse, label *them* as bad or inconsiderate, enlist the age-old technique of changing your perspective.

No matter how horrified you are by someone else's behavior, remember that their behavior is inherently neutral (unless, of course, it causes harm to others), and it is your reaction that is loaded with emotion. Their behavior might be different from what you would have liked or what you would have done, but that's all it is—different. It is not bad, wrong, or atrocious; it is you who have placed yourself in the position of judge and jury and labeled someone's behavior (or the person).

If you are having a visceral reaction to someone's behavior, before you choose to react based on that reaction, note that the emotion is coming from *you*. If, after considering their intent, you conclude that it is obvious that they were malicious and meant to hurt you in some way, find a productive way to express that. But most of the time, if you consider intent as well as the possible origin of your own initial reaction, your perspective changes and you embrace the reality that different doesn't equal bad or wrong.

Ditto for Opinions

What is true for behavior is true for opinions. We all have them and we don't always agree on them. The productive, positive tack is to simply agree to disagree. The far more common tack is one person accusing the other of being bad or wrong because of their opinion. We all have preferences and we are entitled to have those preferences. We want others to respect ours, so we should respect theirs.

> *Karla doesn't like the taste of tomatoes. Or cauliflower. And she gags when she even thinks about the smell of brussel sprouts. Oh, and she's a vegetarian. Her husband, Daryl, calls her "picky" and he doesn't like going out to eat with her. He "can't stand" the way Karla orders her food at restaurants and thinks she is "annoying when it comes to food."*

Let's examine this all-too-common situation for a moment. Is Karla actually "annoying?" According to Daryl, yes, but what Daryl means is that *he finds her behavior to be annoying to him*. That is not the same thing.

And think about this: Why would Daryl actually allow himself to not enjoy himself because of the food preferences of his wife? He makes it sound as if she terribly wronged him somehow. (After delving into this topic with Daryl, I discover that he feels self-conscious at restaurants and he thinks Karla makes a scene by asking a lot of questions when she orders and ordering everything "on the side." So the truth came out: Daryl felt embarrassed by Karla's behavior. He said that *she* embarrassed *him*.)

Meanwhile, the unexciting reality is that Daryl and Karla have different preferences when it comes to food and they should acknowledge that and move on to more important issues. There was no malicious intent; she merely wants the food she is paying for to be cooked the way she likes it. Once Daryl focused on her intent rather than his own feelings of embarrassment, he was able to shed his victimization and enjoy a good meal and the company of his wife at a restaurant.

The Eighth Key
Give What You Want to Get

I am a firm believer that we would all be much happier if we were less preoccupied with what others can do for us and more concerned with what we can do for them. The previous key raised the issue of age-old concept of The Golden Rule: doing unto others what you would want done to you. In this key, I'll explore an important strategy you can use, starting right now, to bring more happiness into your life.

Don't be Fooled by Simplicity

Give What You Want to Get is my favorite of the easier-said-than-done keys to greater happiness. Conceptually speaking, I don't recall ever hearing anyone object to this key or call it hogwash. That's probably because it is such a simple concept that we have heard, time and again, in many different ways. But don't let that simplicity—or the repetition fool you. Just because something is simple, or you've heard it a thousand times and you agree with it, doesn't mean it has become part of your life.

When it comes to taking steps in your life that reflect giving what you want to get, we humans tend to be masters at finding excuses *not* to do it *this time*. My observation—and something tells me that you share this observation—is that it is very easy to do unto others when all is going your way. But when your path has become a bit rocky, or when you believe that someone has mistreated you, doing unto others suddenly takes on the scale of moving mountains.

A Crash Course in Giving What You Want to Get

The most effective, efficient way to make your life a happier one is to take the emphasis away from your happiness and instead try to make other people happy. "*But how am I supposed to know what makes other people happy,*" you ask? It's really very simple. Let's go back to you for a moment. What makes you happy? I'd venture to say that you appreciate it when people listen attentively to you, communicate honestly with you and are considerate of your wants and needs. I recommend making a list of the qualities that make *you* happy. Then, make it your mission to be the embodiment of those qualities.

Now, don't get me wrong, I don't recommend an attempt at an overnight overhaul. But I do recommend taking one quality from your list and thinking about that quality for the week and looking for ways to be that quality.

For instance, and this is a difficult one I admit, let's say you really appreciate it when people listen attentively to you. For the next week, then, begin the day thinking about listening. And each time someone you are dealing with opens their mouth, listen. And I don't mean just don't talk—I mean listen. And if you don't know how, think of one person whom you feel really listens to you. When that person is listening, what are they doing? What do their eyes look like, what does their body language look like and what does it say to you? Visualize your good listener model each time you think you should be listening. Model that person's behavior. Learn to be a good listener. Then proceed to the next quality on your list.

After you've taken a long look at how you like to be treated and then modeled your desirable behavior, it's time to look at some not-so-uplifting stuff: your faults. I know, I know, you don't have any faults. Neither do I. But if I search my long-term memory, I do think that at *some point* in my past someone *might have* commented that I can be a bit impatient. Actually, I *am* impatient at times; I confess. And I'm pretty sure that you can muster up a short list of faults if you really try (ask your partner or your mother if you can't think of anything).

So take the #1 fault from your list and think about when that fault tends to flare up. Write down a couple of situations that trigger it. And for the next week, pay special attention to those situations and to your behavior when they occur. For example, when I have to deal with anything remotely bureaucratic, I tend to become irrationally impatient. So for a week, I decide to be patient. Just like that. I recall my mother and the seemingly unending store of patience she has. I know how I feel when someone is patient with me. It feels good. And I can decide to spread those good feelings.

Step Outside of Yourself

So there you are, *being* pure patience, understanding, judgment-free, or whatever quality you strive for most. Now step outside of yourself for a moment and step into the shoes of those who are observing you being patient, understanding, or judgment-free. How does it make you feel?

Don't You Like You More?

After you've contemplated and modeled the qualities you want to embody, you will notice that you will begin to like yourself more. You'll be proud of your behavior and you'll find self-improvement a most fulfilling exercise. You'll be happier, I guarantee.

And your happiness—and your self-improvement—won't go unnoticed. Good people like to be around good people. The best way to attract great people to you is to be a great person.

Be the Person You Want to Marry

I have several clients and friends who do not have love mates but who are desperately searching for them. My advice to all of them, and to you, is to forget about the search. My advice is to *be the person you want to marry*. And this advice works for work relationships (be the person you want to work with), friendships (be the person you want as a best friend) and even family relationships (be the father you want to have).

When you become the person you want to marry, work with, etc, you will find that you will begin to attract people who are more in line with what you want. Sure you will falter, have moments of insecurity and weakness, and meet people who will test your new patience and understanding. But the more you are able to act in ways you admire and value and not let them get the best of you, the fewer people like that will come knocking at your door.

Do No Harm

Regardless of what is on your personal list of desirable qualities, this is one that everyone should live by. Now, you might be thinking: Tell me something I *haven't* heard. But I have learned that many of life's epiphanies happen not when you hear something new, but when you truly understand—for the first time—something you've heard dozens of times. Do no harm. Think about what these three simple words mean to you.

I'll tell you what they mean to me. No matter what your religious or spiritual beliefs are, no matter whether you believe in heaven and hell, karma, or some other kind of system of retribution, one thing is clear: You don't have to worry about any kind of cosmic payback if you do no harm. So remember this: Do nothing that would cause physical, spiritual, financial—or any other kind of personal harm—to someone else.

> *Barbara's spa was closed for renovations so she went to a local nail salon for her pedicure. She had just begun soaking her feet when the pedicurist asked the client next to Barbara, whom Barbara recognized from her spa, where she was from.*

The woman, who didn't seem to recognize Barbara, began telling the pedicurist about the spa-in-renovation, in great detail. She knew all about the staff's personal lives, including marital infidelities, and she was privy to the financial status of the spa and its owners. Without even glancing around to see who was in earshot or lowering her voice so others couldn't hear, she talked about the intimate details of the lives of people who lived in the same town.

This kind of exchange happens all of the time; it's called gossip. I am here to tell you that, regardless of the rationalizations you will hear from people who gossip, gossip can be harmful, and it is unnecessary at best.

Most of us will be put in the position of choosing whether or not to speak about the details of the lives of others many times in our lives. If you are ever unsure about how to handle yourself, just flip the situation around and ask yourself if you would like your life to be the topic of conversation.

Doing No Harm: A Shortcut to Happiness

Choosing to do no harm is no guarantee that unpleasant things will not happen in your life. In fact, I can guarantee that unpleasant things will happen. But doing no harm does do one thing vital to this discussion: it makes you a happier person.

In addition, the choice to do no harm is the choice to do something positive, which is a great thing to do. Recall that I suggested phrasing all of your goals as going toward something positive. For the best and fastest results in this instance, include a plan for how you will get there. For instance: I wish to become a more peaceful, loving person, and I will work toward this goal by becoming a better listener, compromising more with my spouse, and calling my mother for no reason at all.

I admit that this affirmation is probably simpler in theory than in practice, and it is also a bit vague. But if your list contains items that aren't defined, do some research and define them. Although "becoming a better listener" isn't precise, as I suggested before, you can closely observe someone whom you think is a good listener and do what they do. You can also:

- Ask those around you how you might go about improving your listening skills.

- Get some books on listening and study them.

In other words, if you need to improve something about yourself and you don't know how to go about it, don't stop there. I promise you that you will not improve at anything unless you define exactly what you need to do to consider yourself new and improved. You cannot recognize improvement until you know what it looks like: until you have defined it.

Today's result is often not a result of today.

Life is largely a cumulative experience. But because humans tend to prefer instant gratification over the more delayed variety, we often overlook the meaning and the power of even the smallest acts of kindness (or meanness).

Improving or creating any behavior and being able to sustain it is a process that takes months, if not years. Betterment is a process that doesn't end, because by nature none of us is perfect. And we never will be. But we can be better.

Today's result just might have been coming for a long, long, time.

I am a firm believer that what goes around comes around, and when it does, it has usually gained in both mass and velocity. It behooves you to work, each day, at becoming the best you can be. Over time, it becomes easier and your rewards will seem bigger and clearer. But it is difficult, at first.

If you believe in *karma*, you believe that what is happening to you now is the result of many lifetimes of living. Each time you return to this planet, you replay many of the same scripts and meet many of the same people you have been dealing with for centuries. The objective for each lifetime is to learn the lessons that you haven't managed to learn yet, and you will keep running into the same obstacles until you do.

Now if thinking beyond this lifetime is not something you are comfortable with, think of the concept of karma in reference to a much smaller time period: this lifetime. Is there an obstacle that you have hit, time and again, in your life? Or how about a situation that is not particularly negative or positive, that repeats itself. Has that happened? And haven't you thought it a bit uncanny when it kept recurring?

Coincidence? I think not.

I submit that the entire scenario is not a series of coincidences. In fact, viewing it as coincidence is just a mechanism for avoiding the real issue. And guess what happens when you avoid the real issue? It keeps coming back, over and over again, until you acknowledge it. In order to avoid revisiting negative, uncomfortable, or just plain unproductive situations of any kind, you have to act with intent. I say this because if anything unpleasant is recurring in your life, what you are currently doing evidently is not working. (Likewise, give yourself a pat on the back for drawing positive people and experiences to you.)

The Solution? Create a Plan and Stick to It.

Acting with intent means that you have thought about

what is—or could be—wrong, what your role is in it and what you can do to better it. The solution is to create a plan to better yourself (thus increasing your happiness) and stick to it.

Let's break it down into some smaller parts and examine them separately. My only caveat is to remember that no part of your life exists in a vacuum; all of the parts are connected. The first part of creating your plan is to explore:

- Your family relationships
- Your work relationships
- Your relationship to God
- Your relationship to your Reality

When I say explore, I mean assess the current status of these relationships. How happy are you with them? In what way are you less-than-satisfied or unfulfilled? The best way to improve anything is to determine the ways in which it is not working well. The doubly helpful thing about determining what is not working well, is that you also determine what would make it better. From then on, your strategy is simply one of giving what you want to get.

The universe has the uncanny ability to bring you exactly what you are acting like you want. If you don't want to be judged by others, stop judging others. If you want happiness, give happiness. Live happiness.

Just because you have the right, doesn't make it right.

It is my observation that we as a people are becoming increasingly selfish. We talk about our "right" to do certain things and be certain ways. And certainly, granting equal rights to each of us is essential to the health of our nation. But what I'm referring to here is rights that people take at the expense of common courtesy.

This seems to be most obvious in driving situations. I was driving with a friend of mine recently and he was tooling along in the far left lane (known as the *passing* lane) of the freeway going about 55 miles an hour. As we rode along, a number of cars came up behind us and then pulled to the right to pass us – often shooting annoying glares over at us. I was curious why my buddy Steve was driving in this lane at this speed.

> *David: "Hey Steve – it appears there are a lot of people going around us on the right – why not scoot over a lane and let them use this lane?"*
>
> *Steve: "Why should I? I have a right to be in any lane I want – and I am doing the speed limit. If those guys want to break the law by going faster – then they can just go around me!"*
>
> *David: "Well, sure, you have the right to be in this lane, but it is inherently safer for everyone if the faster traffic is confined to one lane – rather then people moving in and out of lanes. And since the lane to the right seems to be moving at a speed that is sufficient for you – why not move over and make it easier for the other folks?"*
>
> *Steve: "Oh yeah – like they do anything for me! I like this lane and I'm staying in it."*

I think this is a good example of the kind of thinking that does little to make our world a better place. If we each wait for someone else to take the first step in being courteous, we will all be constantly waiting. While it is important that you tend to your own needs, you should not do so in a way that ignores others.

Be generous – not necessarily in big ways – but in everyday living. Let the person with two items go in front of you in the store. Let the person in front of you on the road make that turn into your lane – even if you have to slow down a bit. Smile at the clerk who is short-tempered and wish them a better day. Life is series of everyday, tiny interactions. Make each one of them positive and pretty soon they'll add up to a happier life.

The Ninth Key
Communicate

When I asked a buddy of mine to look over my initial outline for this book, she said, "It looks great, David, but if I may say, I find it surprising that your discussion of communication comes at the end." My response? "If your attitude and your thinking process are off kilter, no amount of communication advice is going to help you."

If you have read this book in order, you have probably noticed that the keys build on one another. (And if you haven't read it in order, you probably made your own connections that are just as valid.) Please indulge me in reviewing my personal process for a moment.

- Once you have embraced the reality that happiness is indeed a decision, you are left with a choice:

- If you are not happy, then what you're doing isn't working. Your choice is to continue to do what isn't working, or to do something else.

- Deciding to do something else essentially means that you are choosing to change. But just because *you* have made that particular choice doesn't mean you can make it for anyone else. You must accept others for who they are and for the choices they make. You might not like who they are or the choices they make, and that's okay. But thinking you can change someone (and make them more like you want them to be, perhaps?) is hopeless and often destructive.

- The only person you can change is you. That's good news. And what's even better, you can choose to recreate yourself at any time. And, in fact, if you are doing it right – you are constantly recreating yourself! You'll have your hands full trying to change yourself. Taking someone else on takes energy away from an area where you really can make a difference, and puts it towards an exercise in futility.

- Changing your attitude includes realizing that life might not always be fair, but it is reasonable. Not every inconvenient or even horrible thing that occurs is occurring to you. Sometimes random things happen and you just happen to be there when they do. Whatever the circumstance, think about what lesson you can learn from it, and move on. And if you played a role in the circumstance, own up to it, promise to do your best to never do it again, and move on.

- Choose your words carefully when you speak to others as well as when you are talking to yourself. Words have an energy and a life of their own. And when you use them inappropriately or carelessly they affect what occurs around you as well as inside you.

- Before you react to someone's words or behavior, consider their intent. We all say things we don't mean sometimes. And we all have judged someone based on their behavior. But think of your own behavior. I bet you think some people should cut you some slack sometimes.

- If people should cut you some slack, you should do the same for them. Whatever it is you want from the world, you should try to give the world. Giving what you want to get is about doing selfless, thankless things for those around you. A friend of mine once said, "Giving is often doing something you totally don't want to do, and with

> no hope that anyone is ever going to find out, track you down and reward you for it." Fortunately, there is a universal law that says that what you put out you get back, in abundance. Put love and happiness into the world, and you are bound to get a bunch back.

The above review of the first eight keys is really a demonstration of The Ninth Key: Communication. I was attempting to clarify what I have been saying to give you another opportunity to understand it. And I have repeated several phrases, verbatim, because repetition helps you move items from your short-term memory to your long-term memory. And I used a little story to introduce it (and throughout the book) because some people learn better through dialogue and anecdotes than through straight prose. And I have addressed you directly throughout the book and used everyday language, so you would feel like I'm in the room sitting down next to you, looking in your eyes, speaking to you alone.

In other words, I have examined the medium I am working with, and I have designed a way of working with it that increases the chances that you, my reader, will get my message. I have made some assumptions about your likes and dislikes (e.g., I don't know you, but I am wagering that you prefer a concise book to a lengthy one. I am also assuming that you'd prefer that I stay away from swearing and profanity). And I have used examples and stories from my own life and the lives of my friends and clients, because they are real and you can probably relate to them.

Communication is an Intricate Process

I believe that the biggest problem most people have with communication is that they aren't thinking enough about what is involved in the process. And I can't fault most people for that; I don't think I learned how to communicate until I was an adult. I deal with adults all of the time and some of them have no idea how intricate the process is. No one told them. No one told me.

In grammar school and high school we all learned things like vocabulary, grammar and punctuation. We learned how to write and we learned how to read. But we learned how to write our ideas on paper and we learned how to read books. Most of us did not learn how to effectively discuss *our ideas and feelings*, and probably few of us learned how to read *people*.

So why is communication so intricate? Because it involves more than one person (i.e., when you are not talking to yourself). And what's the big deal about that? Well, think about your own life. Think about the communication baggage you have. Think about the words you detest, the words you like to hear, the tone of voice that grates on you, the facial expressions and gestures that comfort you, and the facial expressions and gestures that annoy you.

I could go on and on. (If you would like to read a great book that describes the various aspects of communication, I recommend going to www.amazon.com or calling 800-788-7654 and ordering *Communication Essentials*, by Ronni Burns.) The point is that there are so many details about your personal communication style, preferences and dislikes that I can't even enumerate all of them. And then there are all of the memories you have about communication, all of which can be triggered at any time. For example, the look in your boss' eyes reminds you of the look in your mother's eyes when she was disappointed with you. Or you are nervous and you hope that you don't stutter the way you did when you gave your first presentation in front of a large group. Memories of what occurred in the past affect, and in fact frame the events of the present.

Try for a moment to conceive of how many details about communication are unique to you (or so you think), and then multiply that number by two. That is the number of details that you, ideally, would have to know about in order to have the most effective and efficient conversation with *just one other person*. Oh, and by the way, you probably don't know much about the details of the other person. When you really think about it, it's amazing that we every get any communicating done at all.

What to do . . .

As you can see, the process of communication is a complex one, but that doesn't mean you have to make it complicated. Here's my process for how to handle the details and increasing the probability that what you mean is what your listener hears.

Speak Up!

It may sound painfully obvious, but if you don't speak up and let others know what you are thinking and feeling, you cannot later blame them f*or not knowing what you are thinking and feeling*. Remember Mandy and Terrance from way back in The First Key? Mandy was angry with Terrance for not helping her around the house, but she never told him that she was angry or why she was angry. Her comment to me was: "I shouldn't have to tell him."

Though it may seem unfair to you, my belief is that you cannot expect people *not* to cross your personal, imaginary lines in the sand unless they know where they are. You are responsible for letting people know what is unacceptable to you. If you don't, you cannot blame them for offending or upsetting you.

Figure out what you really want to say.

Before you open your mouth, I suggest pausing to contemplate what it is you really are trying to say. In the perfect world, what is it that you would say in the particular situation you are in?

How does your listener process information?

This is different from what you want to say, because this is where you begin to consider your listener. For instance, sometimes I can't tell my sister exactly what I mean, because I know how sensitive she is. She is a person who needs a certain delivery in order to be receptive to something new, or particularly to something she might not want to hear. So I do what I know will make her relax and be comfortable with what I have to say. If I don't, then:

1. I am being self-centered because I am not considering her feelings, and

2. I am completely defeating my own purpose because if I don't consider her feelings, she probably is either not going to hear a word I say or completely misunderstand me. In other words, it doesn't pay to ignore the preferences of your listener; you are just creating more problems for yourself. Your objective is for the listener to be able to process what you are saying based on his/her reality. That is more important than you saying things in a way that is easiest for you.

Listen

Even when you are speaking to someone, you should never stop listening to them. Even if they aren't saying a word. Though the sound of your voice and the meaning of the words you say are important parts of any communication, there are silent variables that are just as important.

When you are speaking you should pay careful attention to what the body language of your listener is saying. You can find dozens of books on body language and reading people in your local bookstore, and this book is not taking on that colossal topic. But my belief is that if you really do listen, your intuition will tell you what you need to know about *your listener*.

For example, is the person moving away from you or toward you as you are speaking? What does your gut tell you that means? What do you think listening looks like? As you probably guessed, if someone is looking in your eye, nodding a couple of times, slowly, and moving toward you, they are probably listening. This means there is a good chance that you are being heard.

On the other hand, if someone is staring blankly at your face, nodding quickly over and over again (maybe they're waiting for a good opportunity to interrupt you and they are not listening well at all), tapping their foot frantically and sitting with their arms crossed over their chest, guess what?

The examples may be a bit extreme, but my point is that we are all emitting continuous streams of signals to those around us. Even when we don't speak with our voices, we are speaking volumes with our eyes, faces and bodies. Be cognizant of how others are acting when you are speaking and, with equal importance, be aware of how you are acting when others are speaking to you.

Don't Take Words Literally

A client of mine, who is a high school English teacher, is a big fan of the correct usage of words. She is forever annoyed with her students for their use of slang and for what she refers to as their "linguistic laziness." She doesn't like when words are added to the dictionary just because enough people misuse them. *Irregardless* is her favorite example of this phenomenon. So many people thought it was a word and used it as a word (meaning *regardless*, oddly enough) that it actually became a word and is in the dictionary at this very moment.

She is what is known as a *purist*. She wants everyone to speak English the way it is supposed to be spoken—according to the rules. As you might imagine, hers is a very frustrating life. It is frustrating because she has an expectation that is so far from reality that she has actually set herself up to experience unending disappointment. No one, except maybe another English teacher who is also a purist, could ever live up—or speak up—to her high standards.

When you are listening to someone else, and this is especially true if you have an above average vocabulary or facility with words, do yourself a favor: Don't take every word literally. If you do, I am guaranteeing you right now that you will never have successful relationships. Don't be so hard on others when they misspeak (use the wrong words) or when they miscommunicate (say something other than what they meant to say); it's hostile and antagonistic.

Instead, listen carefully, let them finish, and then begin to explore what they really meant. When it comes to conversations that are important and that you want to make sure you understand, it is wise to paraphrase what you believe the other person meant, and ask if you are on the right track. It takes just a moment and it lets them know that you care enough to listen carefully and clarify what is being said.

What to do When You are Angry, Upset, or Driven by Some Other Emotion

Unfortunately, timing is everything. We would all prefer to say what we want to say when we want to say it. And get the reaction we would like, of course. But again, that is not a realistic expectation.

If you are so angry at your husband for not doing the one thing you asked him to do on a weekend where he seemingly had absolutely nothing to do, screaming at him on Monday morning as you are both late and on your way out the door to work is not a good idea. Frankly, if you want the depth and breadth of your anger to be heard and responded to, blowing up the moment it arises is almost always counterproductive. The wiser choice is to wait until you are in a more reasonable mood and he is in a position where he will be receptive to what you are saying. In other words, don't try again Monday evening during the fourth quarter of Monday Night Football.

Please don't take all of this to mean that when you are upset in any way that that emotion is not important. It is. But the reality is that there is such a thing as a good time and a bad time to communicate your feelings. There is a good time for you, a good time for your listener, and then there is the compromise: something that isn't perfect, but that you can both live with.

The Last Word: Compromise

A conversation with one person screaming at or talking at another person is not a conversation. That's more like a monologue. Remember that a conversation involves at least two people (although we all talk to ourselves and as long as we are using productive language, that's fine). Both people are there to:

1. Express themselves and

2. Understand what the other is expressing and maybe

3. Respond to what the other is saying.

If number 1 or number 2 is missing, there is no conversation.

And whenever you are dealing with a sensitive topic, think about how, when and where you will broach that topic. Your goal is to be understood, not to say what you want to say. Compromise is something that should always be a part of your thinking when you are relating to another person. It demonstrates that you are considering their thoughts, feelings and preferences, and that you are not thinking in a straight line to what you want. And the more you compromise, the more you find others will compromise, as well. Remember, Give What You Want to Get.

The Tenth Key
Believe

Believe in what, you ask?

God.

Yourself.

The value of all of your experiences.

Believe in God

God, Creator, Higher Power, Supreme Being. Jesus, Yahweh, Allah, Buddha. Whatever moniker you use, your belief in what I happen to call God gives you energy, support and love. And it can be accessed at any moment of any day: whenever you need help, whenever you need centering, and whenever you just want to say *thanks*.

There is more to you than a body that takes up physical space. In the larger scope of things, your body is merely a vessel that carries around something far more valuable—your spirit. I like to think of it this way: Your spirit is a little piece of God. When He was making you, He whispered His love into your soul. And lucky you, you get to carry around that love wherever you go.

What I am talking about is true spirituality: your own personal relationship with God, however that manifests itself. Being spiritual is about living a life that honors your soul. What I am *not* talking about is religion, which implies a connection with an organization that follows rules and has its own rituals and requirements for membership. You can be spiritual without being religious. And some people can be disciplined members of religious organizations without having much of a personal relationship with God.

For me, people devoted to religion but not to God are hypocrites. Many *believe* in false prophets, and many are false prophets. The problem is not that they believe what that they believe, but that people are listening to what they are saying. Do not listen to or abide these people, for they will lead you astray.

But Remember, it is Just a Belief

Just like your opinions, your religious beliefs are yours and you are entitled to them. No one has the right to call them wrong or bad. Some fundamentalist sects of the world's religions believe that if you do not agree with them, you are damned, and will not be saved. The mainstream religions of the world, however, all believe that the most important thing is to believe in God and worship Him. How you choose to go about that is your decision, and it is no better or worse than anyone else's.

Believe what you want, but remember—it's a belief, not a fact. Just as you want others to respect your religious/spiritual beliefs, you should give others that same recognition and respect. If someone's religious practice differs from yours, be happy for them that they have a relationship with God.

For instance, when you are speaking with someone whose beliefs are different from yours, talk about all of the wonderful things you have in common! After all, most religions are based on the same premise: Don't take any action that causes harm to another person. The rest is a lot of rituals that vary from religion to religion. Talk about your similarities, talk about your differences, and respect people who hold different beliefs just as you want them to respect you. Give What You Want to Get.

And when you are *observing* someone whom you know does not have the same beliefs as you do, try not to think about their beliefs. Instead, focus on the person and their behavior. If they are kind, generous and thoughtful, their particular religion is irrelevant. Likewise, if they are not, it is not because of their religion.

Further, if you do not like their behavior, try not to extend that opinion to every person who belongs to their religion. Very few people are spokespeople for their religions and you should always separate individuals from the group. The same is true for race, ethnicity, sexual orientation and even political affiliation.

Believe in Yourself

You are a gift from God. When you truly embrace this notion, believing in yourself should be easy. Although I write a lot about choices in this book, none of those choices would be possible if God didn't put you here to begin with. God gave you free will; the rest is up to you. I am convinced that it is when we lose sight of God that our free will gets us into trouble.

Remember the Eulogy exercise from The Fourth Key? You created your future self: the person you want to be remembered as. From this moment on, you can choose to behave in a way that is consistent with how you want to be remembered. If you believe that God knows you can do it, your belief in yourself will spring from that knowing.

And if you believe that God has knowledge of you always and never leaves you, you know that it is your responsibility to honor Him—and yourself—by doing no harm. Always. There will be many times in your life when you will be able to do things that are not right without ever being caught. It is easy to do the right thing when people are watching you. But it is how you behave in those moments when only God is watching that determine what happens after you're gone.

Spend less time focusing on whether or not you are going to get to Heaven. Instead, spend more time focusing on behaving in ways that contribute to creating Heaven on Earth by the choices you make, your level of active consideration, your attitude, your actions and reactions. If you do this, I have a strong belief that the afterlife will take care of itself.

Believe in the Value of All Experiences

My dear friend and mentor, Peg Armstrong, once told me that there are two things in life: joys and lessons. In line with this theory, I have concluded that personal growth seldom takes place during times of contentment. It is when you are unhappy, stressed, or pushed, that you get creative and begin to see all of your possibilities. Whether your sudden burst of creativity comes from a choice you made that put you in an uncomfortable spot, or whether a choice someone else made put you in an uncomfortable spot, *unless you want to remain there, you'll figure a way out*. These moments are life's lessons, and you should never underestimate them. Sometimes, they can simply change your direction. At other times, they can dramatically change your life.

I believe that the universe has a force of its own that intends to support your personal growth. It sends you experiences that—if dealt with correctly—will result in leaps in your personal evolution. Many of these experiences will require you to be uncomfortable before you are able to grow. In order to take full advantage and learn the lessons the universe has to offer, experiencing unpleasantness is often necessary. But think of it this way: without these difficult situations, none of us would ever evolve.

Furthermore, I have an addendum to Peg's Joys and Lessons Theory: Although you might think that a particular experience is unpleasant, what you *don't* know is that it could have been a lot worse. The real story could be that the universe has actually provided you with the *least* unpleasant path to your lesson. And if you believe that, you will view all of your experiences as positive, productive and valuable.

The Journey is the Destination

We often spend so much time worrying about where we want to go that we lose sight of where we are. To concern yourself with doing what is necessary to get to Heaven (or whatever wonderful place you believe is waiting for those who have lived good lives), is to miss the point of life on Earth. God has given us the ability to create Heaven on Earth by how we treat others and ourselves.

This—your life right now—*is* the destination. God has already done His part. What happens now is a journey that is in large part up to you. And that journey is composed of the myriad choices you make each day.

So if you want to make your Earth into a Heaven, ask yourself how you can make that happen through your choices. Don't ask God for what you want. Instead, ask Him for what you need to make the best decisions and to get through whatever situation you are in. Ask Him:

"God, help me to use the brain you've given me,"
rather than "God, give me an A on this test."

"God, help me to stay focused,"
rather than "God, help me win this debate."

"God, give me the patience to deal with my mother and to hold my tongue rather than lash out with it,"
rather than "God, make her see how right I am and how wrong she is."

God is not like Santa Claus. You don't ask Him for what you want to be delivered to you the following morning, wrapped in pretty paper with a bow on it. I believe that God has already done His part in creating you, blessing you and letting you know that He is always with you if you need Him. Your job is to make the choices that will make Him proud.

In addition, your job is to thank Him, everyday, for everything He has enabled you to do. Learn to say, for example:

"Thank you for the opportunity to help me learn patience."

"Thank you for giving me the free will that I will use to make positive, productive choices that help me take control and live a happier life."

A Final Thought

It is my hope that these *10 Keys To Taking Control and Living A Happier Life* will prove valuable to you as you begin to incorporate them into your life. Your daily happiness is the totality of many moments where you are presented with a choice: to harm or not to harm, to say something nasty or to say something nice, to judge or find common ground, to see the negative in people or to see God in them. I encourage you to begin to make more productive choices today – for today is all we have. Join me in making the most of it!